SOLID GROUND *of* BEING

A PERSONAL STORY OF THE IMPERSONAL

ART TICKNOR

TAT FOUNDATION PRESS

Solid Ground of Being
Copyright © 2009 by Arthur R. Ticknor

TAT Foundation Press, 47 Washington Avenue #150,
Wheeling, WV 26003. Website: *www.tatfoundation.org*

Cover design: Luke Roberts

Cover photo: San Rafael Reef, Utah, by Bob Fergeson. See
Bob's photo site at *www.NostalgiaWest.com*

Cover fonts: Felix Titling, Vivaldi, High Tower Text
Text fonts: Palatino Linotype, Amazone BT, Printers
Ornaments One, Life BT, Felix Titling, Vivaldi

Main entry under title: Solid Ground of Being

1. Spirituality 2. Self-Realization 3. Philosophy
I. Title

Library of Congress Control Number: 2009937464

ISBN: 978-0-9799630-5-6

Table of Contents

Like each person who awakens to the wholeness of essential being, each item in this book is both a self-contained topic and a reflection of the whole.

1

The
Turning
Point

The Solid Ground of Being

*F*or many years I believed myself to be something solid standing on something solid.

Then one evening when I was thirty-three I found myself walking on air. Literally. For several minutes all the sensory data coming into my brain, or the mind's projection of that data, told me that my feet were not touching the ground as I walked. I wasn't using drugs, legal or otherwise, hadn't drunk any alcohol, and had no physiological explanation.

That evening started me on the path of looking within to find my essential self, the unknown subject of my subject-object universe. The more I looked and pondered on what I saw, the less solid I became and the less solid the world became. Then another evening, twenty-six years later, I found what I'd been looking for.

A few years later it occurred to me that one way of describing what I found was a solid ground of being—*the* solid ground of being. It's beyond the ability of the mind to imagine and beyond the ability of the mind to describe, and that's because it's beyond the mind.

Beyond the mind we have returned from the realm of the personal to our impersonal source. We can then use our personal experience to speculate on how a fellow human being can make a similar voyage of discovery, to inspire another with a possibly unimagined possibility, and to encourage another to persevere.

Where Is It?

*W*here is the solid ground of being? Very close. Closer than you can imagine. The treasure house is not across the globe, across the street, or even across the room. And we know that the realm of the mind is anything but solid. But that's going in the right direction. We back away from whatever we can see until we come to the very center of the spiral of being—the source of observing—where all problems are resolved.

A retrospective note: My intention with this book was to make it a companion to contemplation by keeping each entry to a page or less. I mostly succeeded until nearing the end of the book, where I wanted to leave you with some detailed, practical suggestions.

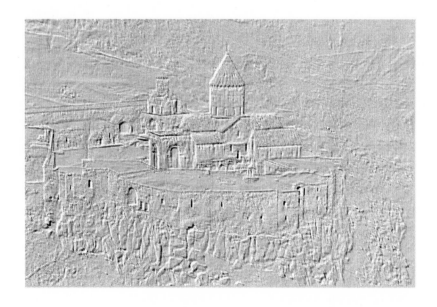

Nkosi Johnson

I heard an interview on NPR in 2004 of an ABC newsman, Jim Wooten, who had just published a book about a boy he had met while investigating the AIDS epidemic in South Africa. The boy's name was Nkosi Johnson, and he had died in 2001 at age 12. The year before, Nkosi had addressed the International AIDS Conference in Durban.

At the end of one of his last meetings with Nkosi, Wooten said he could see that the boy was exhausted, so he decided to cut the interview short. But Nkosi reminded him: "Wait just a moment, Jim. You haven't asked me about death." He went on to say that while he didn't want to die, he was not afraid of dying. Nkosi then left Wooten with the mantra that he'd developed for himself after he learned he had AIDS:

"Do all you can with what you have in the time you have in the place you are."

Is there any better guideline for investing our lives in pursuit of our innermost desire?

Muddled Mind Sonnet

*D*on't be afraid of poetry. (I say that in case you have an aversion to poetry as I did until my thirties.) There are things that can be expressed better in poetic form than in prose.

> Where do I look for X, the Great Unknown?
> How do I tell the false way from the true?
> A rishi says it's Here and Now, Alone —
> To see this for myself, what must I do?
>
> How do I look for X, whatever the cost?
> It's nearer than the mind, another says.
> How do I find the One that's never lost —
> Turn inside out, or flip, or spin sideways?
>
> What is it that I really, really want?
> Can I trace the yearning back into its source?
> Or is the rich, soft longing just a taunt —
> To keep the sled-ride on its downward course?
>
> Where hides the X, the Eye that never sleeps?
> What veil or trance this separation keeps?

I wrote this sonnet in 2001, expressing my frustration at having no perspective on where or how to look for that undefined, unknown essential self after more than twenty years of introspective searching. In retrospect, it was an accurate assessment. What we're looking at is always an object of consciousness, while what we're trying to find is the subject of consciousness. It's a nasty conundrum with no *apparent* way out.

Last Supper

I wrote the poem below about the same time as the preceding sonnet. I was getting together with some friends for a weekend retreat, and when I asked myself what I hoped the results would be, what came out was a new insight into the pain of unending transience, of continuing arrivals and departures. It also produced a foreshadowing of the actual transition to knowing the self—a form of knowing that is unfamiliar to the mind. To contrast it to the mind's knowing, we could describe it as unknowing. Actually it's a direct knowing, a knowing by becoming one with.

> Surrounded by friends one last time,
> No more arrivals or departures.
> Movement ceases,
> Silence prevails.
> A solitary tear
> Halts on its downward journey.
> Sorrow blends into joy.
> Knowing melts into unknowing.
> Color recedes with the observer.
> Anxiety fades into Peace.

The existential pain of individuality comes with the conviction of separation. The individual—a thing apart—can never become whole. Becoming whole requires transcending individuality, which turns out to be much ado about nothing, since individuality is in fact nothing more than a very convincing belief or dream.

Turning Point

*T*he turning point for me came unexpectedly. In fact I didn't even recognize it as such at the time. And it wasn't anything I did or can take credit for, although I suspect my persistence after I no longer could remember why I was persisting may have been a factor.

It descended as a subtle change of mood or conviction. In retrospect, I finally became serious, and it occurred while I was on a solitary retreat—one of many I'd done over my years of searching for the self. Three months earlier I'd read something that triggered the recognition of a desire to get more serious than I'd ever gotten before. The fuse had been lit.

At times in the past I had experienced inner changes that occurred as if a mental switch had been thrown. This time there was no such noticeable demarcation. Sometime during the middle of the retreat the unwitting attitude of a lifetime changed. I was no longer content with knowing things conceptually. I had to look for myself, to see for myself. The door to looking back at what I was looking out from had opened—and I felt impelled to distinguish what I could confirm, by looking, from what I previously knew or believed.

This direct looking led to the recognition of the final opposition between what I could see I was versus what I believed myself to be, and the continued looking at that contradiction burned out the resistance to "becoming" that which we always have been and ever will be.

The Question Is

*H*ow can you see something new? If you're at the point where you can admit you don't know yourself, and if you feel that knowing yourself holds the best possibility for a permanent, total answer to the misery-aspect of individual existence—a big set of ifs—then you're faced with the question of how you can see something new: How can the self see itself?

The individual self exists in a domain of duality. Subjects (the self, for example) only exist in relation to objects (not-self). That's the domain the individual has to work within until he can transcend it. There is therefore no direct way to go about seeing the self.

A botanist can see something new by hunting for a flower he hasn't seen before. But to see what a flower really is, he may have to look at it with the eye of an artist. His curiosity to do so may be released by admitting to himself that he doesn't really know what's behind that which may be familiar.

When we look with curiosity and some detachment, it may become obvious to us that everything we see—whether it's people, places, our fingers and toes, our thoughts and feelings, and so on—appears on an unknown viewing screen within our consciousness. It's as if there were a TV somewhere in our brain. (No one has ever come across one while dissecting human brains as far as I know.)

Although the mystery of *where* we see remains undetermined, there's only one place to look for something new, and that's at the screen upon which all thoughts and things appear.

One and the Same?

*W*hat are you looking for? Is it love? Security? Pleasure? Approval? Beauty? Self-esteem? Truth? Harmony? Home? Satisfaction? Purpose? Meaning? Completion? Comfort? Ease? End of Anxiety? Eternality? Something other?

+ Have you ever asked yourself "Why?"
+ If you attained it, where would that leave you?

What are you running away from? Emptiness? Emotional pain that threatens to be overwhelming? Fear that threatens annihilation? Terror of introspection, of looking within, that threatens to tumble you into the abyss of the unknown? Fear of social ostracism that threatens an end to existence as you know it? Something else?

+ Why?
+ What is it that's so unsatisfied and yet so fearful?

Have you ever considered the possibility that what you're really looking for and what you're really running away from are one and the same?

Seeing Something New

*W*e may see many new things on our viewing screen, but we're not looking for newness *per se*. We're interested in finding the self.

We can't force new sights to appear on the viewing screen, but we can remind ourselves about what we're looking for—and then turn our attention away from thoughts and things that don't relate to our objective. In fact, anything that appears on the screen is precisely not the self; it's an object in the subject's consciousness.

Where does that leave our search? Fortunately, as introspective looking brings into view more and more of what we had assumed was the self, the hypnotic identification with those *attachments* becomes weakened. We can see our torso, arms and legs—so they are not the essential self we're looking for. Going further inside, we can observe our thoughts and feelings, and even mental processes such as decision-making and introspection.

This process of going within is like peeling layers off an onion. We may eventually arrive at the point where the only attribute we can assign to our inner self is that of awareness: We feel that we're an aware *something*, an observer. There's nothing left on the viewing screen that we can identify as self. We're seemingly stuck, like Sartre, with no exit.

But what about the viewing screen itself, the background upon which all the thoughts and things appear? What is it, this screen of awareness?

Seeing Something New, recapped

The question is: How can you see something new? The context is the individual who admits he doesn't know himself and who feels that knowing himself is the best shot at a permanent, total answer to the suffering side of existence. The *koan* behind the question is something along the lines of: "How can the self see the self, which it hasn't yet seen or recognized?"

Does seeing something new mean that you have to see something that you've never seen before, or does it mean you have to look with a new eye? Is it a question of something new and unfamiliar appearing on the viewing screen, or is it a question of a new way of looking?

In either case, all thoughts and things appear on the mental viewing screen, whatever and wherever that is. So all looking is in that direction.

Does the observer have a way to influence what appears on the screen? Not directly. (I'll save the subject of *will* for later discussion.) But by reminding himself what he's looking for then watching attentively, he can "turn his head" away from irrelevant thoughts and images. Doing so with some frequency and effort may bring a series of revelations—about what is not the self.

When we ask ourselves what we're looking out from, and when we actually *look*, we see it's that aware space or screen upon which all thoughts and things appear. What we're looking out from is aware—without any help from you or me. It's awareness. The Awareness. Self-aware. "But wait a second," we say to ourselves, "I'm a separate something that's aware of it—"

If the mind stares at this vast contradiction, something has to give.

The Formula

*I*f there's a formula for self-realization, for discovering the solid ground of being, it eludes me. In retrospect I have a conviction of what blocks such realization, but I see no defined set of steps that an individual can follow. Each person is built up from a unique combination of genes, disposition and experience—and that combination has to be worked with in order to be transcended.

The ground of being is beyond the personal. And there's the crux of the problem. How does a person go beyond individuality?

I have several friends who have "made the trip" and are working, both individually and together, to help others. As far as I know, that's an unusual situation—possibly unique. Their personalities and their life-stories, including their paths to self-realization, vary widely. The common denominator, other than the fact that most shared the same teacher, Richard Rose[1]—is in what they found. The way they go about working with others varies according to their own life-experience. And the disparate personalities provide great evidence for what personal traits may be most helpful in the search for self. I'll get back to that later.

Each person who wants to know the self must take the trip himself. A teacher or helper can't "pass it on" or do it for him. The searcher must reach a point where he becomes his own authority, looking and seeing for himself.

---

1   See the TAT Foundation website tatfoundation.org for more information on Richard Rose and his teaching.

2

Always Right Behind You

Always Right Behind You

*Y*ou may have a hard time believing this, but the self you're looking for is never not with you. When we consider the possibility that whatever created us hasn't deserted us, the closest we can imagine is the mother-child connection. It's different, however; the mental umbilical cord is still attached, and the Self communicates through a silent language of mood.

> *I am always right behind you*
> But turn around and you won't see me.
> I am never not with you —
> Why aren't you always with me?
> I am at the center
> while you stay at the periphery.
> I am there, too,
> but you won't find me there.
> When you turn round
> the center stays behind you.
> Stand still while turning your gaze around
> and look at what you're looking out of.

Ultimately, knowing the self involves the surrender of individuality. We may have to struggle and fight internally to arrive at that point. It seems to come with more trauma for some than others, probably depending on how much the sense of self, the individuality sense, has been chiseled away by life's shocks, by honest introspection, and by time's erosion.

Subtraction

*T*he ground of being is discovered by the conscious mind becoming aware of its source. It can't be done directly for a variety of reasons but has to be backed into— a subtractive process in the words of Richard Rose.

We believe ourselves to be a separate something— often coupled with the belief that whatever created us has become disconnected from us. The truth is more like the Egyptian symbol of rays radiating from the sun, each ending with a hand:

Backing up the ray of creation is equivalent to a detachment from faulty beliefs about what we are. That letting-go occurs through shocks and abrasions provided by life and by our efforts of self-inquiry.

Possibility & Inability

*M*any people are motivated to look for certainty out of a fear of death. One of my friends who succeeded in the quest said his last question or *koan* was whether there was some part of him that was permanent.

I was never much worried about that angle. Until my thirties I felt that death held out the best hope for an end to the suffering side of life. That was based on the possibly naïve assumption that the lights would go out and I would cease forever. As I became a little more psychologically sophisticated (read: self-honest), I admitted that I had no idea what death would bring—and that it might be more-of-the-same or even worse.

Recognizing that death wasn't an automatic get-out-of-jail card became a contributing factor in my search, but the primary motivator for self-definition was a longing for wholeness, for completion. I felt that there was an unassuageable pain of separateness, and I believed that there was a possibility of transcending or going beyond individuality. How to actually go about it became more frustrating the longer I worked at it.

Whether your motivation appears to be on the fear side of the emotional spectrum or on the longing side doesn't make any difference as far as I see it. Either can lead us to a total answer if we persist.

Persistence, however, depends on faith in the possibility of finding a final answer—an answer that goes beyond belief to Absolute Certainty—and in many cases on overcoming or outlasting our belief in our own inability to go there.

Back to Basics

"*G*ive me something concrete to do," she said. Oh, boy ... where to start? Defining the self— answering the "Who or what am I?" question, also known as becoming one with Truth, with Reality, and so on—is the most abstract pursuit on earth. And yet it has to be carried out with common sense balancing intuition.

It's a way of living your life aimed at understanding that life, as Richard Rose would say. And there's no cookie-cutter procedure for stamping out self-realized people. It's a highly individualized pursuit, each person being like a lock with a unique combination.

If you're really serious about it, consider the following program:

1. Admit to yourself what you want most from your life—one goal or accomplishment.
2. Make that deepest desire that you're aware of your #1 priority in life. Don't kid yourself if you think you can have several #1 priorities. You'll be tested to find what's most important to you (see *Sophie's Choice*—a 1979 novel and 1982 movie). If you "don't know," then make its discovery your #1 priority. Don't let lesser desires, or fears, interfere.
3. Become your own authority. Use thought, but go beyond it. Use feeling, but go beyond it. See for yourself.

If you're fortunate enough to run across a self-realized person, don't let your fears or prides get in the way of asking for help—for as long as it takes you to accomplish your objective.

Man to God

*C*ould you say it a little louder,
Could you repeat it again?
I didn't quite hear you,
or I didn't quite understand.

I'm trying, Daddy, I'm trying
but I'm oh so confused—
I thought you sent me out
to stand on my own, to become a man.

Isn't there something I have to accomplish,
some errand I have to attend to,
to win your approval? You mean
it's okay to come home again?
Now?

I believe you, Daddy,
but I'm so afraid—you can see
how wobbly I am. If I try
to look around I'll lose my balance
and fall.

I can make a wide circle
and come round in that way
but then I'm still out here
and home is still behind me.

Could you say it a little louder,
could you repeat it again?
I feel like I'd better keep peddling
while I figure it out....

Permanent Happiness

"*I*'m confused ... don't know what to do ... unhappy," he told me.

"What do you want to accomplish with your life?" I asked.

A: I don't want to accomplish anything ... just make it through with as little pain as possible.
B: Like death row ... no hope for escape ... make the best of a bad situation?
A: Yes ... pretty poor, huh.
B: What's the number-one thing you want from your life?
A: Permanent happiness.
B: What do you mean by "permanent"?
A: Until the end of my life.
B: And by "happiness"?
A: An end to the roller coaster ride of ups and downs.

What he's asking for isn't that difficult to attain. The ups and downs he's talking about are mood-swings that reflect our hypnotic identification with feelings. Admittedly it's a little more challenging to get some detachment from feelings than from thoughts, but effort put into an "effortless" form of meditation, such as *vipassana,* can end the enslavement to mood-swings. (Don't worry, not the end of emotions or changing moods themselves.)

But his definition of "permanence" indicates an underlying belief that he is something that was born and is going to die. Even if he finds some comforting belief about what death will bring, he hasn't found a *permanent* solution to his problem—because he still believes his current self, what he currently is, to be impermanent—and that thorn will still be stuck in his side.

Surrender

*L*ooking back over my life, there were three occasions where I completely surrendered my sense of control.

The first occurred when I was maybe 10 or 12, on an excursion with my father to see how the deer were faring during a tough winter in upstate New York. We decided to use skis rather than snowshoes, and we got into a swamp where we sank up to our armpits in the snow. I remember having given up with exhaustion, and I had no memory of how my father got me out.

The second time was when I took my first swim in the Pacific Ocean and got caught in a rip tide, which I'd never even heard about. I felt myself being pulled out to sea and flailed desperately until my arms and legs just wouldn't work any more. At that point I relaxed (to my retrospective amazement), figuring this was it. I lost all sense of my body and the ocean, and I began getting a life-review, as if my consciousness were traveling back over my life from earliest to more recent times. Later I felt my knees scraping on sand and found myself washed up near shore maybe a quarter mile from where I'd been.

The third occurrence was in May 2004, at age 59, on the last night of a solitary retreat—when I relaxed after an intense but effortless period of mentation and self-inquiry over the preceding week. This time the hypnotic identification with the mind loosened, and I found myself at the core of my being, beyond life and death.

My feeling is that at the point of surrender the aperture of the mind opens to the extent that our state of being or self-definition allows—from blackness to lesser illuminations to total self-realization.

Oasis in an Arid Land

*W*e are drunk and yet still thirsty.

Our inebriation stems from various stimulants and depressants, from the outer—sensory intrigue—to the more interior, such as conceptual thinking, imaginative visualization, and feeling-addiction. Some of us are more besotted with the outer world, some with the inner. And there's a potent interplay in most cases. I remember a university student, for example, who said he chose the school because they had a good football team. He was an ardent fan and said his association with a university that had a winning team gave him a sense of self-worth. And that's what we're all about, isn't it—our sense of self-worth.

We're afraid to sober up, fearing that we couldn't stand the clarity of truth. So we keep ourselves tipsy. But satisfaction and fulfillment continue to elude us. We're headed toward death, and despite any comforting beliefs we're desperately clinging to, deep inside we know we're missing the great treasure that life has to offer us.

There's an oasis in this arid land, whose water quenches the thirst and heals our sightless eyes, revealing the source of eternal life and love. When we smell the water, we're near. When we see the oasis, there will be just one final inebriant to overcome: the subtle and bewitching conviction of individuality.

Do Not Fear the Darkness

*D*ylan Thomas, knowing that his father was dying, extruded his feelings into a poem that ended with the lines:

> *Do not go gentle into that good night.*
> *Rage, rage against the dying of the light.*

Do they resonate with your own feelings?

There is no need for fear.

My velvet blackness removes all cares,
dispels all vulnerabilities,
terminates all threat
without and within.

Immersed in me emptiness is filled,
longing is finally answered,
permanence is found.

Here, and only here, is love complete,
mother, father, mate, child, friend perfect.

Only when you have lost your self in me
will you find what you've been looking for.

Control

A friend told me that he'd asked himself a question about what to do, and the answer that came to him was to ask a guru he respects for advice and enact the suggestion, whatever it was. Then the fear hit him.

He didn't ask himself about the fear but turned his head away from it, so his mind didn't hunt for words that would give his intellect a conceptual explanation.

What I believe he saw was the reaction of the ego, which was determined not to give up its sense of control, real or imagined.

The individuality sense—the belief that I'm a separate something that is continually threatened with being overwhelmed and that if I were to let go of the sense (or pretense) of control, things would rapidly descend into chaos—is the keystone in the arch of faulty beliefs about the self that keep us in the dark as to our real state of being.

When the ego steps aside, temporarily relinquishing the sense of control, it does so only when swept off its feet by love or, in extremity, because it sees no option. Depending on its degree of bloat, the letting go in the latter case may be traumatic and seem like death itself. Unless this occurs during physical death, the ego function cranks back up when awareness resumes its projection into body-mind consciousness. But the mind now has a conscious contact with its source, and our identity no longer becomes lost in the mind.

3

Skating on Thin Ice

A Koan

*H*ow can the self see the self, which it hasn't yet seen or recognized? How can I find my self? I'm going to go back over some material I covered earlier in order to introduce a question that has no conceptual answer.

Do I look for a never-before-seen thing to appear on the viewing screen, or do I look for a new way of looking? There's only one viewing screen, so regardless of what I look for, it has to appear on that screen. Do I have a way of influencing what appears on the screen?

By reminding myself what I'm looking for (i.e., the self; the same self that I'm reminding?) then attentively watching the viewing screen, I can turn my head away from irrelevant thought streams. If I do this with some frequency and energy, I may get some revelations (*satoris, eurekas*) that speed up the process of peeling off the layers of not-self.

Eventually this "me" who's looking for his real self may get to the point where all the attachments—arms, legs, thoughts, feelings, mental processes, etc.—have been stripped away ... having been seen as objects of consciousness, leaving the *subject* as a still undefined (unknown) individual awareness. At that point I may realize that nothing that appears on the screen of awareness can answer my question. All those things are either outside the self I'm looking for or inside the self—not the self *per se*. Where do I then look to find the self?

Is the essential self beyond the realm of limitation— including the law of the excluded middle? *If all things are outside me* and *all things are inside me, what am I?*

Will

*T*he question of *free will* comes up in religious and psychological investigations, and the equivalent question of *doership* arises in philosophy.

J.J. van der Leeuw provided an excellent analysis for a conceptual understanding of the question about free will in a chapter of *The Conquest of Illusion*. Richard Rose, from direct observation of the mind, described will as "a reaction to react in a fixed, planned reaction" in his *Psychology of the Observer*. In other words, we have witnessed a pattern of action in certain circumstances and we react with determination to change the pattern when those circumstances arise in the future. If the reaction pattern changes according to our wishes, we then say we have exhibited will power.

What I think free will means to most people is the freedom to do what they want when they want. The opposite could be termed imprisonment. Varieties of imprisonment include:

- Being locked in a room you can't get out of.
- Having conflicting desires that can't be satisfied.
- Not knowing what you want. (Uncertainty.)
- Fears that impede the satisfaction of desires.
- Not choosing the desires in the first place.
- Procrastination.
- Addictive or obsessive habits.
- Being stuck in space and time.

The belief in doership is simpler to investigate yet harder to dislodge. There is plentiful evidence of our being an agent of thought and subsequent action, but claiming to be its principle cause rests on the argument: I didn't see anyone else doing it; therefore, I claim the title.

SOLID GROUND OF BEING

Skating on Thin Ice

I was reading a while back about some men who had gone to the Yukon during the Klondike Gold Rush. In the springtime they were traveling south by dogsled on the Klondike and the Yukon rivers because they could make much better time than going by land. But the temperature was rising, and the ice was getting thin. They could hear it cracking and could sometimes see water beneath it—so they were under constant tension. They had to keep moving to minimize the chance of breaking through the ice.

That's how we live our lives. The threat of death is constantly hovering around us once we become self-conscious, and we have to keep moving lest we break through the thin ice under us and….

The thing we fear above all else is stillness. We equate non-movement with death. We have to keep busy, physically or mentally. The only break is during non-consciousness, which is why sleep and some forms of meditation are so refreshing. But they are temporary, and we return to the scorpion-sting of consciousness.

Is there no way out? Is the only solace to be found in some reassuring belief about what death will bring?

Personal Traits

$\mathcal{A}$re there some personal traits that are necessary or at least helpful for self-realization? If you've been fortunate enough to encounter a living guru, you may assume that whatever traits he exhibits are the ones required for success. I know that was my conclusion—and it provided a good excuse for self-pity, since I knew there was no way I was ever going to be like the guru.

There are several people I've known for years, some for decades, who have now navigated the grand odyssey of self-knowing to a successful conclusion. I knew them for at least as long before their realizations as since, and I initially thought it would be easy to isolate a few traits that they shared in common, which I could then relate to you. But as I compared these friends in my mind, there was only one trait that occurred to me that they all held before enlightenment (and afterwards), and that was the value they placed on friendship.

Some people, maybe most, *use* friendship to advance their agendas, but what I'm thinking about is a *love* of friendship. We may not be fully capable of loving our friends unselfishly while we're still under the spell of an individuality-sense, but we can love the ideal.

When we love the ideal of friendship, we see the ugliness of wanting to take advantage of another person and the beauty of wanting for the other the best that life has to offer. Finding friends to work with on the quest for self-realization and truly valuing their success lessens the grip of what prevents our own success.

Taking the Bull by the Horns

 he spiritual path, the path to knowing the self, is one of overcoming a fear of looking at something we perceive as a threat to ourselves. It's like we're being chased by a raging bull that's intent on doing us in, and we're panicked into trying to escape from it.

If we're unhappy and feel we know what to do about it, then it's merely a question of paying the price—generally in terms of overriding any conflicting fears or desires. But if we arrive at the conclusion that we don't know ourselves well enough to know what will bring lasting happiness, then we're faced with a thornier issue. And if we're fortunate enough to feel that only a full self-knowing or self-realization will do the trick, then we're coming up against the biggest problem that life has to offer. How could we attack that problem productively?

We can look for advice and inspiration from others who have preceded us—and it would be self-defeating not to do so. But simply following someone's advice is likely to be more running from the bull. So what's an alternative?

We need a strategy, and it will need to be refined as we go. We need to stop running from the bull long enough to take stock of our not-knowing situation and devise an action plan. We may find ourselves making all sorts of excuses for not doing that, but those are more running from the bull.

At some point, if we're going to pursue self-knowing productively, we need to take the bull by the horns.

Aphoristics

*E*nlightenment, or spiritual realization, is *completion.* There are two categories of human beings: incomplete and complete. Enlightenment is the transition to completion.

The solution to one's essential discontent, suffering, or disease is the *death of delusion.* Our existential suffering rests on the conviction of individuality. The solution is the demise of that delusion. When that occurs, the Unmanifest recognizes Itself through its manifestation.

God is the eye that sees itself. Nothing is hidden from that eye.

There's no oneness as long as there's a me.

We just have to *look* within until we become our own *reliable* authority.

The deepest longing behind all longing is for what's actually the closest of all.

By letting go of pretense, the I expands to fill and swallow space-time.

The Call

*T*here's a mute child within
    Who tugs on our attention,
Trying to overcome our need for noise,
Pulling us into our courage center
Where matter condenses back into light,
And we find ourself ...
Enthroned in Silence.

Regardless of what you're looking for, you won't find a satisfactory level of it until you discover what you really are ... and when you do, you'll find satisfaction beyond your greatest imagination.

    Complete Satisfaction equals the end of suffering equals knowing the Self. Knowing the Self occurs by *observing what's observing*.

    Observing what's observing implies becoming a mirror reflecting the light of awareness back on itself. What is your attention focused on: Personal preoccupations, plans, desires or fears ... or Awareness?

You, Consciousness & Awareness

*Y*ou are conscious.

You know that you are conscious (i.e., you are self-conscious).

You are aware that you are conscious. Are you conscious of Awareness?

Consciousness depends on Awareness. It comes and goes, is turned on and off like an appliance powered by Awareness.

While you are identified with consciousness, the mind, I-amness, you do not know the Self.

There's a resistance to knowing the Self that has to be burned out or blown out by the same unknown force that powers consciousness. That resistance is a faulty but very sticky belief about what you are.

You are what's aware (i.e., awareness).

You are aware that you're aware (i.e., self-aware).

Awareness is self-aware.

There is only one Awareness, not two or more.

You are That. Tat tvam asi.

4

Jesus on the Bus

Truth Issues Forth

Truth issues forth from the Self
     as true and false.
Love issues forth from the Self
     as love and hate.
Now issues forth from the Self
     as before and after.
Space issues forth from the Self
     as here and there.
Silence issues forth from the Self
     as sound and quiet.
Identity issues forth from the Self
     as self and other.
Being issues forth from the Self
     as existence and death.

The Self is beyond true and false.

The Self is beyond love and hate.

The Self is beyond before and after.

The Self is beyond here and there.

The Self is beyond sound and quiet.

The Self is beyond self and other.

The Self is beyond existence and death.

Heart versus Reason

Q: "Can you give an explanation of 'seeking with the heart' vs. 'seeking with reason'?"
A: There is only one way of seeking, which is the way of seeing.

*W*e're in love with—*love* is being identified with—our bodies, until we eventually intuit that they're not us. We're in love with our mental patterns, especially our self-images, until we eventually see that they're not us. We may see what we really are but not accept the implications, remaining in love with ourselves as a separate seer, a thing apart from the source of seeing. This progression of seeing generally comes in bits and pieces spread over a long period.

It's not clear that we can do anything to hasten the process or insure that it comes to fruition. But since there's no proof that we can't, it makes sense to try. The nature of that trying depends on the patterns that have developed and the associated memories that make up our personality or individuality.

The direct way of seeing is looking. If we can't do that, then we do what we think is most likely to result in looking. Depending on our personalities, that may take the form of "seeking with the heart" or "seeking with reason."

Jesus on the Bus

S trangely enough, since I wasn't a traditional "believer," the most moving and memorable dream in my
life featured Jesus. This occurred when I was 40 years old,
during a month-long solitary retreat. The dream began
with me waiting at a bus stop for Jesus (the logic of which
I didn't question). As a bus pulled up to the curb, I could
see through the side of it, and I saw Jesus recumbent on a
bus seat. "Jesus is dead," was my shocked reaction.

But as the bus came to a halt, Jesus stood up, and I
boarded the bus. He didn't look like any picture I'd ever
seen of him, but there was no doubt in my mind who he
was. His hair was reddish orange and kinky. His face was
exceptionally pale, freckled, and clean-shaven. He had a
jewel hanging along his nose from a hook, like those used
to hang Christmas tree ornaments, on a lower eyelid. I
don't recall looking at his eyes.

He wore a coat or robe that was deep purple—silk,
I think—with a lozenge-shape pattern in the weave. He
took the robe off, and I saw that it had a bright orange,
gauze lining. Two points I should mention: the first is that
most of my dreams are in grayscale, and this was one of
my most brilliantly-colored dreams; the second is that I
later read that the word *gauze*—a thin, translucent fabric
with an open weave, originally made of silk—derives
from Gaza (southwest of Jerusalem) where it was woven.
Beneath the coat was an unbelted, plain tunic the color of
oatmeal—made of linen, I would guess—that looked like
it would be very soft to the touch.

The bus stopped. We got off and went into a building, where we entered an empty auditorium and sat on
the edge of the stage with our legs dangling down. Then
Jesus spoke the first and only words in the dream: "Arthur,

everything is going to be okay." My first reaction was surprise that he knew my name. Then I began sobbing. I awoke sobbing, and whenever I recalled the dream that day or for some days afterward I would begin weeping again. I had no idea why.

A month later, my father died unexpectedly. I didn't even know he was ill. And it surprised me—since I was a grown man with a family of my own and didn't feel emotionally attached to him—to realize that one of the two foundations of my self-image was no longer there.

Reviewing my journal sometime afterward, probably months later, I saw that his death had occurred exactly thirty days after the dream. And I then realized that the dream was somehow an attempt by what I'll label an inner intelligence to prepare the outer man. In order to do that, it had to find an image that would trump the father in the child's mind (that is, emotionally). And having been brought up a Methodist with Sunday school lessons as a child, the one symbol that could do that was Jesus.

A Fork in the Road

$\mathcal{O}$ nce upon a time there was a man who was trying to serve two masters.

But because of that, neither one could count on him.

So they asked him to make a choice.

Are You Moving?

*W*hen you're looking out the window of a plane, watching the shifting scenery below, are you moving—or is the scenery moving?

Conventional wisdom says "both": it's true that the earth is spinning on its axis (and wobbling in its orbit around the sun), but the plane is moving in its arc over the earth's surface. Yes, but what about you? Are you moving? Conventional thinking is that yes, I'm sitting in the plane that's moving, and therefore I'm moving along with the plane. But are *you* moving?

When you go for a walk, are you moving—or is the scenery moving? Well, this is more clearly a case where I'm moving (you may say), although some of the "scenery"—people, vehicles, clouds and so on—is clearly moving, too. But I can see my legs and arms moving—and without that, the scenery wouldn't change ... well, wouldn't change as much ... the background wouldn't change ... or at least not as fast. Okay, but are *you* moving?

If you're imagining or remembering or dreaming a flight or a hike, are you moving? If I'm shifting my position while I'm sleeping (you may say), or yes, as I inhale and exhale.

Are you what you see, or are you what sees?

(What sees a dream? Is it moving?)

He Moves, and He Moves Not

> He moves, and He moves not. He is far, and
> He is near. He is within all, and He is outside all.

The above lines are a translation from the *Isa Upanishad*, and they may be as close to describing the truth of Being as language can get.

The "He" is not some superior Being apart from you. It's the "you" that you really are—not the individual you that you may believe yourself to be, which is something separate and apart.

You may conclude that "He" has two parts, one moving and one not moving. But that's not the case, nor is it a matter of His being in movement at one time and being still at another.

In the mind's way of knowing, the *law of the excluded middle* holds. Aristotle defined this as "... It will not be possible to be and not to be the same thing." But that condition is precisely what the *Isa Upanishad* is pointing at. It's a state of being that is beyond the mind, beyond the duality that comes with manifestation.

You move, and You move not. You are far, and You are near. You are within all, and You are outside all.

Still Life

*D*ream from April 2000: I'm in an old-time general store, in line with other people to pay for purchases. The proprietor, who's waiting on the customers, is an attractive, grandmotherly woman. Her graying red hair—the color that's called strawberry blonde, I think—is swept into a knot behind her head with wisps escaping and touching her cheeks.

As I near the front of the line, my attention is drawn to a young redheaded woman with an infant girl at the checkout counter. The baby is sitting on the counter and reaches out affectionately to the older woman. The conversation between the two women is animated and friendly, joking. Sunlight coming through a window casts a golden reflection of the windowpanes onto the wood plank floor.

The final frame of the scene is like a still picture. Time has stopped, and I now observe my body-self from outside. My friend who's behind me in line has leaned up against me and put his arms casually around me, one over my shoulder, watching the scene and demonstrating his affection for me in the casual embrace. That embrace registered to me (the separated, disembodied observer) to be out of place in the dream-scene and yet nobody seemed to react to it.

As I awoke with this picture in my focus, I realized that the friend was Paul H—a childhood friend who began showing up in dreams during a difficult period in my life. With this realization came the possibility that we were friends in that past era. More importantly, the loosening of identification as a body-self in the dream world presaged its later occurrence in the waking state.

I Have Never Left You

I have never left you.
Your existence depends on my attentive grace at every instant.

I have particularized,
and the particle thinks it is a thing apart.

I have waved,
and the wave feels separate from the ocean.

You and I are not two.

Déjà Vu

$\mathcal{I}$ was hiking along a firebreak on a ridge in the Angeles National Forest circa 1980 when I came around a bend and saw a pond surrounded by lush greenery tucked into a bowl in the dry terrain—and "recognized" it although I'd never seen anything remotely like it in my lifetime.

I was driving on a dirt road in the rolling desert near Tombstone, AZ circa 1985—the first I'd ever been in that part of the country—and had experience after experience of knowing what I was going to see before I topped the next rise.

Driving along the road south of Moab, UT on the way to and from hiking in the Canyonlands area in the spring of 2007, I passed a scene on the west side of the road on two successive days—high desert with sage brush inclining up from the road to rocky hills with openings into canyons—which was hauntingly familiar, although again nothing I'd seen in this lifetime.

Those were three strong *déjà-vu* experiences I've had, and they have always caused me to wonder about an explanation. There is something so arresting and compelling about them and the strong sense of nostalgia that has accompanied them.

I read where an MIT neuroscientist concluded that déjà vu is a memory problem that increases with age. That hasn't been my experience, at least so far. I can conceive of the first and third of the above occurrences being dismissed as possible neural malfunctions, but the second one defies that explanation, since it included a series of predictions that panned out exactly as anticipated. Whose memory was that…?

Host or Guest?

*L*in-chi (called Rinzai in Japanese; died around 866 AD) asked his students if they could distinguish host from guest. What do you think he might have been referring to?

The guest comes and goes; the non-guest, the host, does not. When you read these words, are you the host or a guest? That question goes to the heart of existential comfort or discomfort.

When we believe ourselves to be an individual being, we exist in the realm of Great Discomfort (a.k.a. Hell). To avoid facing the immensity or our malaise, we try to keep ourselves constantly distracted or sedated.

As guest, we play dress-up and imagine: "I am what I wear." We love pretense, imagining: "I am what I see" (the role I'm playing—parent, child, spouse, student, teacher, boss, worker, for example; this body; these thoughts and feelings, and so on). And we take credit as the unseen cause of actions we observe—the decision-maker, the thinker, the doer.

The existential problem arises from the subject-object confusion of the individual as described above. Becoming lost in identification with what he observes, he believes himself to be that which comes and goes—a guest.

The true self, the host, is that which observes—the Great Secret, the only seer that sees itself.

The abode of the host is Heaven.

5

Knowing What We Really Want

Control by Avoidance

A friend who lives in a major South American metropolis has written that he avoids areas where he's liable to encounter street gangs. He knows he could be overwhelmed easily, and he wisely limits the risk. His action is an intelligent reaction to a fear voice.

He writes to ask about a decision he's made to no longer seek enlightenment actively but to restrict his activity to observation—sort of a being-in-the-moment strategy.

There are so many issues involved, such as his concept of enlightenment and what he knows (from interior observation or introspection) of doership, that there's no simple answer. But my sense is that this reaction pattern parallels the one concerning street gangs: maintaining the delusion of control by avoiding fights.

An active attempt to know the self involves a series of fights among the desire and fear egos that constitute the decision-making committee. When we pursue an objective, we align with a particular set of those voices that favor the objective. And whenever that subset loses a battle—which occurs frequently on the spiritual path—it's a painful blow to our individuality-sense.

Enlightenment is the birth of self-knowing that accompanies the death of illusion. The individuality sense, the keystone in the arch of illusion, is constructed to fight to the death for its survival. Not pursuing the objective of enlightenment is an attempt to avoid the fight.

Fate?

A little bug flew in my eye
I presume to get a drink
But it must have been his time to die
Because he made me blink.

What Is Important?

Time is now fleeting, the moments are passing,
Passing from you and from me;
Shadows are gathering, deathbeds are coming,
Coming for you and for me.
Come home, come home,
You who are weary, come home....

From Softly & Tenderly, *by Will L. Thompson*

A re you like a man who's family is running out of food, who needs transportation to get to work to earn money for food ... has $500 for a down-payment, but can't decide what car to buy ... a Ford or a Honda, a 2-door or a 4-door, etc., stuck in indecision over the unimportant, forgetting what is?

A Fourfold Itinerary

*F*irst, discover your deepest desire. That may not happen immediately. In my case it took a dozen years from the time I was getting ready to graduate from college. I knew what I wanted at a feeling level—to become complete, to find Full Satisfaction—but I didn't know what would do it. It became evident to me that I was searching for purpose or meaning, and also that I didn't know where to look. Frustration! Then at 33 I met a man who said, "The answers are within." Euphoria! I'd found the purpose I'd been looking for—the direction to search: within.

Second, make the pursuit of your deepest desire, or finding the direction of it if that hasn't occurred yet, your primary priority. You'll be tested if you do so. Your self-honesty will be challenged repeatedly. Conflicting desires and fears will thwart your efforts. Doubt, procrastination, and forgetfulness will plague your intention. Loved ones, careers, security and so on may melt away.

Third, ask yourself frequently why you're doing what you're doing. Does it support your priority? That doesn't mean you have to keep on the move constantly. Rest and relaxation are important to recharge the batteries. But don't forget what's important to you.

Fourth, eliminate habits that cloud the mind. Don't let yourself be fooled.

What prevents attaining your heart's desire? Not knowing your self. What prevents knowing yourself? Faulty beliefs about what you are. What you truly are is unbelievable. Literally. It's beyond the realm of belief. When you go there, you'll find you're home.

Before: This Camera

*W*here am I, exactly, at this point in time?
     Am I on a path that will bring me home?
What is it that stands between here and there,
     that keeps me split, that separates me from Thee,
          Eternal Beloved?

It can't be a matter of travel in space;
it can't be a matter of passage through time.
Can this view of my self as something trapped in space,
     as something caught in time,
          as some thing,
               be transcended?

Is the path, then, through seeing the self as no-thing?
I've looked and looked and so far have found nothing
     that can be labeled self,
merely pictures,
     still-lives, scattered on the ground.

What remains is this self-conscious awareness,
     this observer,
          this feeling
that I am this camera which is recording,
          and is aware of its recording.

Can't You Say Something New?

I have to laugh when I think about this, because I suspect that people who are familiar with my words must think it at times. As a seeker, I'm sure I was waiting to hear or read a magical sequence of words that would open the secrets of existence to me. And *mirabile dictu* the words of someone who has died to illusion can have that magical power.

Words can precede and trigger direct realization, but it's not the words themselves that have power. It's rather a transmission of the true self, of Mind, to itself through rapport between two of its creatures.

When I was walking today, the words: "Take the fight to the enemy" occurred to me. I've been thinking about nobility of spirit lately, and how two popular writers of western tales—Louis L'Amour and Max Brand—found a formula for keying into that aspect of human psychology. The hero, usually single-handedly, would save himself, or better yet rescue a weaker person or possibly a whole town, by taking the battle to the seemingly impregnable enemy.

The enemy of saving ourselves and maybe some of our-others is a seemingly unassailable gang of beliefs that keep us tied up in knots. Taking the fight to this enemy is really as simple as challenging the beliefs we hold onto about ourselves. We become aware of the beliefs by asking ourselves why we did or thought something, and then we allow honest uncertainty to apply doubt to the underlying belief. The beliefs may be relatively good or bad, but we can't afford to be enslaved to beliefs if we want to become free.

Heaven

*H*eaven
neither travels ahead
nor lags behind
but is always with you.

Simply remove the barriers,
and you're there.
The barriers have no heft,
being nothing other than beliefs.

Beliefs of being right or being wrong
are intermediate barriers.
Beliefs of being something
are the final barriers.

Heaven is the place
of no place, no time.
No thing has ever made it through
the gate between thing-land and heaven.

Knowing What We Really Want

*I*s it possible not to feel *in our bones,* as a friend likes to put it, our innermost desire?

If life is piling success after success on us, that may keep us closer to the emotional surface. Temporarily. But I haven't come across any biographies of people who've attained wealth or fame or mastery of an art or science, and so on, who have found that it was ever *enough.* Gene Autry — "Public Cowboy No. 1" and a thoroughly likeable guy from what I've read of him — was a legend in his own time and was on the Forbes 400 list of wealthiest Americans for many years, and yet he said he'd still be entertaining at 100 if there was an audience.

Any desire implies a want, a feeling that something is missing. There's a great gap, though, between feeling a want and our conceptual interpretation of it. When we interpret a want and say to ourselves, for example, "I want a new car," we've jumped from a perceived need to a conceived solution. We may not have given much consideration to the want itself, which could have been a desire for security (the old car may break down when I'm on the road), for admiration, for status, and so on.

When we perceive a want but can't conceive of what would adequately satisfy it, we may be getting into the depths of the mind. I'm not thinking about a hunger for food and not being able to decide what to eat but of a different sort of hunger — one for which we can't conceive of any category of attainment that would be satisfying.

The deepest desire of the mind is for knowing what we are, and the answer to that desire can't be conceived by the mind. But it is reachable.

51

Depression

*D*epression is a state of mind based on the conviction that what we *really* want isn't attainable.

In my case, I had found my life-purpose when I was 33 and had pursued it rather single-mindedly for a dozen years when a specific non-happening triggered a deep depression that lasted for nearly seven years. The non-event was not receiving a reply to a letter I had written to my spiritual mentor and friend, Richard Rose. When I hadn't heard from him, I sent him a copy of the letter, assuming the original had been lost in the mail. When I still didn't hear back, I concluded that he'd lost hope for me, and therefore that my life-goal was unattainable.

Even though I no longer hoped for my own self-realization, the goal of self-knowing was still my highest ideal, and the following year I moved to Rose's rural property in West Virginia to help keep it available for people wanting to do solitary retreats. Five years later I had a satori-type experience that restored my personal hope and lifted the depression.

Depression is based on a belief, and the belief is based on feeling. Since we can't conceive of what it would take to satisfy our innermost desire, the feeling of hopelessness can't sustain being challenged or questioned. In other words, our *certainty* about hopelessness is misplaced. Nothing can be known for sure until the knower is known, as Richard Rose would point out. Any certainty before that rests on mere belief or wishful thinking.

Our innermost desire might be permanently satisfied at any instant.

Figuring It Out

Q: Is there a process that would help me figure out what I really want?

Like you, I always *felt* what I wanted. A want is a feeling of what's lacking. It doesn't exist unless felt. Conveniently enough, the feeling of want (hunger or thirst, for example) includes the desire to satisfy the want. The deepest feeling of what's lacking is the feeling of being incomplete, of incomplete being.

"Knowing" what we want is a secondary process ... one of translating feeling into conceptual thought. The loudest feeling of want at the moment may be thirst, which the mind then translates into: "I want a drink of water." The organism can then hopefully find its way to a source of potable water. On the way to the water, the organism may encounter a threat to its life, and the loudest feeling of want may become self-defense, delaying the satisfaction of the thirst-want. And so on.

For about a dozen years after I graduated from college I went through recurring periods of deep feeling of lacking purpose or meaning combined with not knowing where to look for the satisfaction of that desire. I think that's generally the type of "not knowing what we want" that people refer to. We feel want; we translate that feeling into thought—which might be worded or pictorial; then we arrive at the recognition of an action to satisfy the want. When I met Richard Rose, I found where to look for the satisfaction of the desire for purpose or meaning to complete me. Something he said rang my bell ... but it took a couple days before it got to the conceptual machinery: "All answers lie within." Then the stage was set for action.

Your Daily Life

*W*hat human being doesn't want to be completely, not partially or temporarily, satisfied in life? However, by the time we're adults we generally become more "realistic," maybe cynical, unless we've adopted some form of wishful thinking about post mortem bliss. But some small fraction of humanity stumbles across the testimony of the rare individuals who pop up throughout history saying that it's possible to find total satisfaction in life. And some small fraction of that small fraction accepts that testimony as the only possibility that offers real hope for a meaningful existence.

A common denominator of the total-answer testimony is that what we're looking for is found by *going within* to discover our true identity or essential being. The personal experience of those offering the testimony differs widely, as do their suggestions and advice, but they commonly point to some form of introspection: going within by *looking within*.

What does that fractional fraction do in their daily lives? If you're one of them, you can answer from personal experience. Do you arrange your daily life so that your routine when waking up includes action toward finding complete satisfaction? The rational human being who hopes to find total satisfaction would begin his day, use opportunities during the day, and end his day with introspection, right? Or would he be too pressed for time when he woke up, be too busy and distracted during the day, not be in the mood when he returned from work or school, be too hungry before dinner, too lethargic after dinner … eventually devoting time to introspection last thing before going to sleep, if at all?

6

The Invisible Hand of Doing

You Could Walk Right Through Me

The waking-state world appears terrifically solid. And yet what do we really know about it? What we "know" are percepts and concepts that appear in our consciousness. About *the world itself* we know nothing directly. When we get right down to it, there's no steady baseline we can use to determine a correct interpretation of our perceptions.

And then we have the dream world, which is every bit as convincing when we're dreaming as the waking world is when we're awake. I had a dream a while back in which I was walking rapidly through a desolate landscape, watching the terrain at my feet. I descended a gravelly path skirting a small hill, and behind me I heard the voice of a friend, KP, saying to other unseen people, "There goes a [some positive adjective, which I didn't recall exactly] man" and then: "I've got to go see him."

His tone was enthusiastic, and I heard him running to catch up with me as I kept walking. When he neared, he started to go around me in order to face me, and I said to him, "You could have just gone through me" (rather than around me, since I'm not solid).

This made perfect sense to me in the dream, where otherwise-opaque walls can be seen through or even walked through. I knew that what my friend saw was actually a projection of his mind. How could that be solid? Why did he walk around it? The projection ("my body") didn't prevent it. It must have been some belief he maintained.

The dream world may be closer to reality than the waking state, reflecting as it does the holographic nature of the universe as witnessed by quantum physicists.

Emptiness

*O*ur deepest complaint
points the way:
Thoughts and things
appear and disappear
from and into the void—
that aware plenum
that self-knowing all-ness
that boundless, non-particularized wholeness
always and forever
our being.

Proud Pretense

*W*hat we truly are
is hidden from the view
only of those who refuse to look.
Refusing to look
is a painful impossibility
since what we truly are
is self-knowing.
Awareness is self-aware.
What causes existential pain & suffering
is the proud pretense
the painful lie
of individual awareness.

Documentary

$\mathcal{S}$uppose you were going to make a movie, whose *subtitle* would be "The Life and Death of [your name goes here]." And suppose there were three possible choices for the *title* itself:

- Pride
- Fear
- Surrender

What are your feeling-reactions to each possible title? How well does each one, when you consider it, describe your experience? And what is the relation of surrender to pride and fear?

What specific occurrences of self-surrender have you witnessed? Have there been surrenders to others? What were the motivations in each case? Did the surrender leave you feeling inflated or deflated? Have there been surrenders to what you might consider lower aspects of yourself? Higher aspects? Did they leave you feeling better about yourself or worse? Have the surrenders been voluntary or involuntary? How is surrender connected with control? Have you willingly surrendered some control to what you might consider a higher principle or power? If so, what did you hope to gain by doing so? If not, is the motivation based on pride or fear? What do you really want from your life, and what would you be willing to surrender if necessary?

Dress-Up

*L*ittle kids love to play dress-up, easily imagining "I am what I wear." When I was a kid, the boys liked to dress up as cowboys or Indians and the girls as princesses or mommies. We love pretense or make-believe when we're children, and we continue with that love affair as we mature. We still feel differently about ourselves based on how we're dressed, but our dress-up becomes increasingly internalized as well.

 The strangest thing about our lives is that we function as if it were normal to know nothing about what we really are. We define "self" in terms of what we're not (other people and things) and define "other" in terms of not being us. We feel that we exist, and we leave it at that. We continue the game of identifying with what we see. I am this body ... I am the role I play in relation to others ... I am these thoughts and feelings.

At a more sophisticated level of make-believe, we take credit as the unseen cause of what we see: I am the thinker, the decision-maker, and the originator of action. It's as absurd as if I opened my front door, found a package left there by an unseen delivery service, and concluded that I put it there.

The Invisible Hand of Doing

*T*he question "Are you the doer?" is equivalent to "Does the sun appear in the east in the morning?" for most people. They observe doing and take credit for being the instigator. A little investigation into specifics might shake their conviction and bring their sense of identity into question—a possibly unnerving experience that most of us want to avoid like sarin gas.

A neighbor behind me has a little girl whom he pushes on her swing. It reminds me of when my kids were little and how they enjoyed those swing rides and how I enjoyed providing the muscle. I'm sure if someone asked me then if I were the doer of that action I would have laughed at the silliness of the question. My arms were doing the action of keeping the swing going. Nobody was making me do it—it was voluntary on my part. Of course I was the doer. Invisible hands of doing? Ha!

If I had looked into what preceded the action, I would have seen that a thought of action had "entered my mind," perhaps in the form of a picture of a past swing session or perhaps at the request of the child, and the physical action had followed. If I had observed closely I would have seen that between the thought and the action there was an interim agreement to go along with the thought and not veto the action.

To take credit for instigating the action, I would have to have instigated the thought that preceded it. I would have to have decided to have or create the thought before the thought occurred. But that's not all. I would have to have decided to make the decision to create the thought before the decision to make it occurred. Do you see where this is leading? It's not enough to say: "I didn't see myself deciding to create the thought, and I didn't see myself deciding to make the decision to create the thought, but I must have done those things." That would be like sitting in an outdoor café chatting with friends, noticing a backpack that hadn't been there earlier leaning against my chair, and telling myself I must have put it there since I didn't see anyone else doing it.

"But I feel like I have something to do with creating my thoughts," you may say. "I certainly feel like I play some role in the thought process." A friend provided a good example: He said that when he notices a song stuck in his head he feels that he has to try to keep it going. Why? Because he fears if he doesn't, thought will stop—and then he will be completely out of control. He might walk into traffic, or who knows what.

Does feeling that something's true make it so? If we're not consciously deciding to create each thought before it occurs, if we're not consciously deciding to make each decision before each decision-making sequence occurs, if we're not deciding what desires and fears will have a say in each of those decision-making sequences, not deciding what arguments will be made before they're made, and so on, then how can we claim to be the initiator of action that results?

The question: "Are you the doer?" is really equivalent to: "Do you make the sun appear in the east each morning?"

Every Moment

*A*t every moment
you are choosing
to go through the revolving door
that brings you back
into the land of ups and downs,
of happiness and unhappiness,
of life and death.
When you tire of the drama
of disappointment,
know that the other door,
the one you've shied away from,
is open.
It takes you back home
to the land of wholeness.
To go through that doorway,
all you have to do is look
in that direction –
which you're afraid to do
because you fear
that it's the abode of death.
We associate death with non-movement.
So you pretend frantically
that you don't know the doorway
is there … here … now.
It *is* the doorway to death,
but to death of illusion
and to completion eternal.

The Problem at Hand

*T*he problem at hand is always very specific: something we want or fear. But we humans tend to leap over the specifics and grasp grand generalities. When there's inner turmoil, rather than addressing the specifics of it we wish for peace, a lack of inner conflict. That's equivalent to looking for rabbits with horns. The mind functions on opposites. Thus there can't be happiness without unhappiness, ups without downs, and so on. Some people jump from the desire for inner peace to the grand solution of world peace—playing god without having god's capacity to keep the wheels turning. So they get discouraged at what a big job it is. All this kind of thing is based on not facing the truth.

The mind, like the world, is not subject to non-perturbation. True peace occurs only where there is silence and non-movement—and that's what the individual considers death. When we accept the truth of what we really are, we find that what we are at the core is silence and non-movement. Since there are no parts to rub against each other, wear out, etc., there is no irritation—only wholeness. Since there is nothing lacking, there is no desire—only complete satisfaction. Since it has never been born and is not subject to dying, there is no fear—only love.

The individual who wants to "go there" has only to allow his will to align with the will of what created him. That occurs when we listen to or feel our innermost yearning. We don't get there by avoiding life. We live our lives aimed at that wonderful alignment, striving for it without any guarantee of success but with the faith that we'll never regret having lived our life that way.

Direction

I had gone to college because that's what people do,
had flunked out my freshman year, and had no direction in life. That summer, when both of us were 18, my
girlfriend got pregnant. Suddenly I had a direction for my
life—and I was delighted. We were married, I went back to
school, and in my senior year I was hit with the first wake-
up call in my life. I was majoring in math with a vague
idea of continuing on to become a professor, I guess, when
it dawned on me that I didn't have any great talent for
math—so it would be a lie to students and to myself. I
remember thinking, in shock, "I'm going to have to get a
job, go to work eight hours a day, five days a week, for the
rest of my life ... what a boring prospect!"

After graduation I got a job in data processing
(big companies were starting to buy computers and hir-
ing math majors to program them), and by the time I was
twenty-nine I had become manager of a data center with
more than thirty people reporting to me and a budget
of more than two million dollars. I had a wife and three
kids I adored, a nice house, cars, all the things that should
have made me happy. But something was missing. On
and off for about a dozen years after graduation I would
go through periods I thought of as identity crises (a good
label in retrospect), looking for some missing purpose or
meaning in my life. But for everything I could think of doing, becoming, or attaining, I could mentally fast-forward
and realize it wouldn't be enough.

Then after a series of more-than-coincidences I met
Richard Rose. I had already read *The Albigen Papers* and
thought him the most humorous person I'd ever read,
but he projected certainty, and I was certain that it was
impossible to know anything for sure (failing to see the

contradiction of my own certainty). I'd also heard about his doing things for no payoff and was highly suspicious of that. So when I met him, I introduced myself and figured it would be good to lay the cards on the table. I told him I knew why I was interested in self-inquiry, saw that it was selfish, and wondered why he was doing what he did. His eyes sparkled, and he said, "First of all what you're doing isn't selfish. And I do what I do because I can't help myself—it's an obsession." That knocked the chip off my shoulder. "This guy's okay," I realized.

After he talked for a while (it was at a meeting of the Pyramid Zen group at Ohio State U), a gong went off inside me—I recall being surprised, not knowing there was such a thing inside me—and the words that formed in my mind were: "This guy's telling the truth; I've never heard it before, but something in me recognizes it." After the meeting we went to a McDonald's in the basement of the OSU student union for coffee and more talk. When I left there, all the data that was coming to my brain told me that my feet weren't touching the ground. I knew then that the phrase "walking on air" was more than a loose metaphor, and other people must have experienced the same sensation.

A couple days later I was scratching my head, asking myself: "What was it Rose said that caused the euphoria?" And it dawned on me that the message I heard was that all answers lie within. I had spent a decade or more scanning the horizon looking for answers, never suspecting that there was an entirely different direction where I could look.

7

What I Wonder

What I Wonder

To set the tone for a weekend retreat with some friends, I asked the following rhetorical questions, prefaced by "Here's what I wonder":

- Why did you come here? (Most of us had flown to Houston, Texas for a long weekend.) Parenthetically: Did you come here, or did here come to you? (This gets down to the question of knowing what the self is, and its relationship to the cosmos.)
- What are you looking for?
- Do you hope to find it here? Parenthetically: And then what? Leave it here? Take it home with you?
- If what you're looking for is here but not where you came from, it can't be that great, can it?
- Why not go home right now rather than some time in the future? Parenthetically: This question applies both practically and metaphorically.

Deeper than Love

There is love, and it is a deep thing
but there are deeper things than love.

First and last, man is alone.
He is born alone, and alone he dies
and alone he is while he lives, in his deepest self.
From "Deeper than Love" by D.H. Lawrence

A friend, who's working on a computer science Ph.D., had a life-changing shock while driving his car about a year ago. All of a sudden he realized he wasn't doing it. The car was being piloted skillfully, but it was all happening automatically. This may not sound very shocking in the telling, but his sense of self was shattered. His previously unquestioned beliefs about who or what he was were thrown into jeopardy, and the disturbance eventually brought him into the conscious pursuit of self-inquiry.

A year later he sees that a successful pursuit of self-inquiry may jeopardize his long-held values, which are based on unscrutinized beliefs about himself. He has become aware of a fear that his Ph.D. may no longer seem important and aware of a complementary pride that he is a person who finishes what he starts. Consequently, he's on the fence about self-inquiry.

What he may not see is the deeper fear of having his current undefined sense of self, which is threatened by self-inquiry, undermined.

Do You Know What Love Is?

William Samuel (1924-96) lived outside of Birmingham, Alabama most of his life, which progressed from that of soldier to metaphysician to self-realized man.

During a weekend retreat he held in Georgia in 1993, which was filmed by PBS, he told about having had an angioplasty after an earlier bypass operation. Everything seemed okay, then the angioplasty collapsed, followed by a collapse of each of the bypasses. His doctors didn't give him any hope of surviving. He was lying in bed still alive when he said he should have been dead. An old lady who came in to take care of him leaned down and whispered in his ear: "Do you know what love is?" He said he was totally honest for maybe the first time in his life and replied, "No. But I would like to." She responded: "It doesn't matter. God loves you, and I loves [sic] you." He said he began healing at that instant.

Do you know what does the work of keeping us alive, or what does the work of bringing us to self-realization?

Rumi, the Persian poet and Sufi master, spouted poetry for hours at a time over a period of years, wearing out in succession three scribes who tried to keep up with him. In one of his most beautiful poems, "The Tavern," he described that he found himself drunk in this tavern (that is, alive and confused) and didn't know how he came here, so whoever brought him would have to take him home.

Love is one of the names for our Nameless Source. Love does the work. Do you know what Love is?

Thinking About Thinking

*A*t the core of our existential suffering is a feeling: a feeling that something isn't right, that we're somehow incomplete.

To find what we intuit is missing in our lives that would make us complete, all we have to do is face the truth. The truth seeker is like a physician who is his own first patient. Is there a best way to think about the diagnosis and the treatment? Where does thinking go right—or, more importantly, where does it go wrong—in the business of truth-facing?

One of the most intriguing stories in *How Doctors Think* by Jerome Groopman (a practicing physician and teacher holding the Recanati Chair of Medicine at Harvard Medical School) is the author's description of his first night in charge of a hospital ward as a new intern. He was chatting with one of the patients, who suddenly went into extreme respiratory distress. Groopman said he just stood there "with an empty head and my feet fixed to the floor." Fortuitously, an out-of-town doctor who was visiting a friend walked by the room just then, examined the patient, and told the author what to do. That was Groopman's first lesson in becoming his own authority. He realized, "I needed to think differently from how I had learned to think in medical school—indeed, differently from the way I had ever thought seriously in my life."

The truth seeker will similarly reach a point where he needs to think differently from the way he has ever thought seriously in his life. Physician, heal thyself.

Truth or Pill?

I heard some dialogue on a TV program — an episode of "Numb3rs," a series about an applied math professor who helps his older brother solve crimes for the FBI — that goes to the heart of the problem. A psychologist was counseling the older brother and gave him this advice: "If you want to feel better, take a pill. If you want to get right, face the truth."

Most of us spend our lives trying to bully or seduce the world into giving us what we want, and then attempting to twist our internal psychology when the world doesn't respond satisfactorily, to make things right. What we try to avoid at all costs, though, is facing the truth about ourselves.

Why is that? Our thinking is the source of the problem — specifically the beliefs we hold about what we are. (The line between thought and feeling becomes blurred when we look at beliefs. Beliefs are feeling-convictions that we often haven't expressed to ourselves conceptually.) In order to face the truth about ourselves, we may need to do a good bit of thinking and feeling about thinking and feeling. How do we go about that productively?

We challenge our beliefs about what we are *by looking at them.* Am I what's seen — or am I what sees, what's aware? Am I this body — or is it an object in my view? Am I these thoughts, feelings — or are they also objects in my view? Am I the doer — do I "do" decisions and actions, or are they also potential parts of the view?

Spanish Mission along the San Antonio River

All Hat & No Cows

I lived in San Antonio, Texas for a few years and really liked the people and the feeling of the area. Fond memories include visiting the Spanish missions along the San Antonio River south of town—especially going into one that was still in use (Mission Concepción I think it was) and hearing the trumpet music of a small *banda* under the central dome welcoming the worshippers to mass; tubing down the Frio (cold) River with friends from work on an idyllic summer afternoon; and getting together with three close friends once or twice a week for impromptu dinners, dominoes and conversation.

Many of the men, women and children in San Antonio wore cowboy hats and boots. There was even one shopping center close to where I lived that had a giant replica of a pair of ostrich skin cowboys boots in the parking lot, visible from afar. I never did acquire either hat or boots but probably would have if I'd been there longer.

Anyway, one of the jokes among the urban cowboys—and possibly a real cowboy scattered here and there—about their more newly outfitted brethren was that they were "all hat and no cows."

There are spiritual seekers like that, too. Have you donned the robe, the meditation practices, and the vocabulary? Have you read the books, hunted the guru, talked the talk? Or have you made an unshakable resolution to know yourself to your essential core, regardless of the cost?

Do You Have a Strategy?

*S*uppose you were going to tackle a project you'd never done before—like building a cabin or a boat. Would you begin by going to the lumberyard and buying lumber that might be good for the project, or by going to the do-it-yourself store and buying tools and hardware you might need?

No doubt if you had determination and persistence you'd eventually complete the cabin or boat, if you lived long enough, but it's not a very productive approach. Of course, that would be fine if your real objective were merely to keep yourself occupied or distracted in your free time, or even to rationalize that you were making good use of your time.

But let's say you had no shelter or you knew a gargantuan flood was coming and survival depended on having a seaworthy cabin-boat. Then you would likely be motivated to complete the project posthaste. And to do so, you'd make a plan.

The plan would be for productive action toward accomplishing the objective in minimal time, which would include intervals of R & R as well as adequate nourishment. If comprehensive, the plan would also include consideration for avoiding extended periods of nonproductivity and other contingencies.

If your goal is finding the solid ground of Being, and you don't have a strategy—what's up?

8

Why Seekers Fail

What Is Your True Situation?

*O*rdinarily, I prefer asking irritating questions to making flat statements, since the questions have a better chance of piercing the ego-defense armor. But sometimes plain assertions can be more shocking. Here's an attempt at the latter:

- You find yourself "drunk in this tavern" (i.e., alive and confused; see "Do You Know What Love Is?"). You don't know how you got here, and you don't know how to get home. You want to go home, but…. [fill in your own rationalization here].
  ~ You have no plan.
- You're in the jungle. A tiger has gotten your scent and is going to eat you. You know that, but you can't quite believe it.
  ~ You haven't grasped the situation, unable to face it.
- You tell yourself you're doing something—maybe even that you're doing as much as you can—and that you'd do more if only you knew what to do.
  ~ There's a story about Arjuna in *The Mahabharata* when he was feeling superior to his brother Bhima because his brother didn't have a daily meditation practice. So Krishna took Arjuna on a trip to the mountain top, to show him baskets and baskets of flowers being carried to Shiva, explaining that they were offerings from his brother's devotion. Arjuna figured if his brother, who never sat down to worship, could produce that many flowers, then his own devotion should produce phenomenal results. But when Krishna showed him a small mound of flowers and told him they were the offering from

his devotion, he was stunned. Krishna explained that his brother didn't limit his practice to once a day.

- You need help (and you know it) but you're afraid to allow it, for fear of losing control. You want to be the one to make the final decisions.
  ~ This shows the need for "doership" introspection. You witness decisions being made and you claim credit for them—without taking an objective look at the processes going on in the mental factory.
- You want to know the truth about yourself ... but not yet.

Ordinarily I'm a respecter of do-not-disturb signs, but if you're here under the flag of wanting to get more serious, I'm going to ask you to do something: touch a hot stove. (Think about it.) Would you do it? Just for an instant ... reach down as far as you can and feel what it is you're wanting ... in want of ... lacking ... missing.

You're dying of thirst, but you refuse to drink. (Why?)

Begin at the Beginning

*E*very day is a new beginning, and it's a good idea to get your bearings at each beginning. Some people do it with devotion or prayer. One of the most effective forms of prayer—if you listen for answers—is asking yourself questions.

Why did I come here? Where did I come from?

What am I looking for?

What's my plan for finding it? Does my life have an intention? Do I have an intention? Are they aligned?

What am I?

Am I something that exists in time—or does time exist within me?

Did I come into this world—or does the world come out of me?

Are the questions of birth, death, reincarnation, life after death, and so on, coming from a questionable perspective, based on questionable assumptions about what I am?

Am I something special? What makes me special?

Am I some thing?

Am I confusing objects of awareness with what's aware? Am I what I observe—or what observes? Do I think and feel—or do I observe thoughts and feelings? Do I act—or do I observe actions? Do I make decisions—or do I observe (sometimes; partially) an interior argument and decision-making process?

What am I at the core of my being?

At the end of each day, do I ask myself how I did today, how the day went?

If there's a tomorrow, will I start off in better shape than I did today?

Now

*J*anuary 2008: A man enjoying himself by sliding down the banister of an escalator in the Hollywood and Highland Center Mall lost his balance and fell backwards, dying when he hit the floor several stories below.

Won't ever happen to you? Are you certain? It seems to me like an apt metaphor for every person's life. Every individual is on a downward slide to death—which is going to come, often unexpectedly, at some "now" moment.

Do you think the escalator-railing rider was prepared for his moment of freefall, able to accept his death with equanimity? Was he ready for his ride into nothingness? Are you?

If you're dissatisfied with sleepwalking through life, it's a question of awakening to your true being during that long moment of freefall from birth to death.

Dying While Living

I don't talk much about death because I know what I am, where I came from, and where I'm going. What I am was never born, has never changed. This knowing arises from dying while living. What dies is not the self but the delusion of what the self is.

Acceptance

*You know, Art, this thing about hopelessness,
depression. I can't seem to get a handle on it. To
be honest, I am stuck in it, and have been for too
long.... I know I've had a resistance to admitting it to anyone or myself, in that it isn't a stoic
masculine thing. But that may be the surface
reason....*

I wrote back to the above friend that I'd given quite
a bit of consideration to depression in the past ten
months or so, spurred on particularly by a young guy who
just graduated from college last spring. He had contacted
me because he had lost his sense of identity maybe a year
ago and felt like he was a zombie, the walking dead, but
couldn't get that identity back. I could see that it was a
severe blow to the individuality-sense in that his previous self-image had been removed like someone doing the
trick with making the tablecloth disappear from a fully set
table. It was actually a step toward self-realization, but he
couldn't see that. He was like the soldier who wakes up
in the hospital with his legs amputated and who becomes
depressed because his self-image has been shattered. This
fellow is convinced that unless he gets back what he's lost
there's no way to move forward with his life.

When I considered it, I could see a parallel with
the situation that I'd been stuck in for about seven years
after becoming convinced that my teacher, Richard Rose,
thought my case was hopeless ... and therefore that there
was no chance for me to attain my deepest desire. Like
the guy with the amputated limbs, there was no way to
recover what was missing. What I can see now is that the
depression was a life-lesson that was being presented to

me, and the lesson had to do with acceptance. When I finally had the "acceptance" satori, where I saw that "from up here (i.e., my view at the time), everything down there (ordinary consciousness) was perfect exactly as it is and was," the depression evaporated. What prevents acceptance of the facts of a situation is pride, and pride is based on faulty assumptions about what we are. When we accept the facts, we bow our head to truth ... true humility.

The guy with the missing legs may find true happiness ... in a way that wouldn't have been likely when he had all his limbs.

True Happiness

*T*rue happiness is beyond happiness, beyond bliss even. It comes not through ever-increasing happiness but through disillusionment.

Illusion is the source of existential misery, and illusion is based on faulty beliefs—most critically, beliefs about ourselves. Accepting the truth is a subtractive process involving unlearning. Nirvana is the blowing out of the keystone in the arch of faulty beliefs about our identity. The final subtraction propels you beyond thought, beyond feeling, beyond individuality.

We find what we are by going within, and we go within by looking within. By attempting to look within, the dividing line between inside and outside moves inward. How do we go about doing that productively?

Jeffrey Tepler, a hematologist and oncologist in private practice at New York-Presbyterian Hospital, said: *"It's hard to think deeply about patients at the moment when you are seeing them. You need to have some quiet time to reflect and formulate a cogent opinion."* [From *How Doctors Think* by Jerome Groopman.] He routinely leaves his office at 8:30-9:00 PM after reading recent medical literature and thinking about his patients. The self-inquirer has to become doctor and patient, and setting aside some quiet time for that each day is essential.

Joe Biden, when US Senator from Delaware, wrote that while spending long periods in bed after two surgeries to remove brain aneurysms: "I was like a pointillist painter who had been so busy making each dot, he hadn't taken the time to stand back and look at the picture emerging on the canvas." [From *Promises to Keep.*] The self-inquirer needs to become painter, painting and critic. To do that, he has to carve out the occasional weekend, week or month to spend time on his own, away from distractions.

Deep down inside each of us is a deepest desire. A desire is a want, a feeling that something's lacking or missing. We all feel it, but we interpret it in various ways: love, security, meaning, unity, peace of mind, and so on.

Similarly, that's where true happiness is found — within. It's your true nature, your *original face* before your parents were born. Sound too simple? That's because the mind loves complexity. The answer has always been closer that your heartbeat, closer than your breath. It's right here, right now … what you're looking out from … what's aware.

Why Seekers Fail

*W*hy do seekers of Self, Truth, Unconditional Love, or any absolute condition, fail to find what they're looking for? Three possible reasons:

1. Failure to feel their deepest desire consciously. Actually we all feel it, but we're afraid of the implications, so we distract ourselves from it. The majestic poem "The Hound of Heaven" describes this human condition with great poignancy.
2. Failure to find and work with a teacher. It isn't absolutely necessary to find a self-realized teacher, but it's immensely helpful. The Guru is always with us, but many of us fail to recognize him when he appears. Ramana Maharshi related a humorous story about this condition from the *Ribhu Gita* about the sage Ribhu and his disciple Nidagha that you can find on the Internet. [A

Story of Sage Ribhu & his Disciple Nidagha (Chapter 26 of the *Ribhu Gita*).]

3. Failure to find and work with fellow seekers. Working with other seekers, in admitted ignorance, provides invaluable mirrors and reminders. There's very possibly an added factor, with the whole becoming more than the sum of the parts.

The self-inquirer encounters periods of no movement. Procrastination, the everyday symptom of being stuck, mostly comes from failure to face our fears. The path to knowing the self is one of facing psychological fears.

Depression is an episodic and stickier form of being stuck. It's like a spa for the bruised ego, the sense of self, after an affliction of failure, rejection or loss. Imagine waking up in a hospital with one or more missing limbs, for example. We become convinced that we aren't going to be able to get what we want, and we procrastinate standing back up for fear of the ego's getting knocked down again.

There's one antidote that trumps all the failure factors, though, and that is simply persistence.

Critical Path to Nirvana

Τhe path to Nirvana is as simple as 1-2-3.

The starting point is dissatisfaction, which can take on many shapes and hues. It may be tied to a fear of what death will bring, for example, or a deep disturbance at the perceived lack of meaning or purpose in your life, or an intolerable doubt that you are what you think you are.

Step #1 is intuiting, or hearing and believing, that all answers lie within. If you're fortunate, this intuition or belief will also include the understanding that you don't find the answer but become it.

Step #2 is turning the focus of your attention around until you find yourself looking at what you're looking out from.

Step #3 is admitting or accepting the implications of what is seen in step #2.

The critical path diagram is theoretically as simple as:

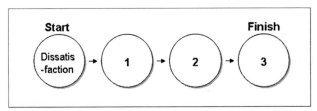

But this process or progression is not something that can be understood by the mind or managed by the individual. Even getting from dissatisfaction to step #1 is not something that we can *do* or force to occur. The vast majority of humanity will not be so fortunate as to reach step #1. [See the September 2004 "TAT Forum" online magazine at www.tatfoundation.org for the rest of the story.]

Simplicity of Being

*T*he Truth is simple and in plain view—"hidden" in simplicity.

There are, however, obscurants. I'll arbitrarily say there are three, all equivalent, like an unholy trinity. One is that believing is not seeing. The belief that Truth can't be simple and obvious gets in the way of seeing. Another is that seeing is not believing. An additional step of acceptance, or acknowledgment, or surrender is needed. And finally, the belief that what sees is not What Sees—in other words, the belief in being an individual observer.

Why are you here? "Why am I here (pointing at the ground)?" can be investigated via psychology and physics. "Why am I here (hands to the sky)?" can be investigated by philosophy.

From a psychological angle, we're moved by desires and fears—two sides of the same coin. You can thank some combination of desires and fears for being here today. Looking at the desire side, a desire is the response to a want, a feeling that something's lacking. The desire to satisfy some perceived need implies the existence of dissatisfaction. Feeling that something's lacking implies the desire for wholeness or completion. That's the story of psychology.

From a standpoint of physics, you could say: "I'm here because I'm not somewhere else. I'm a material body, and material can't be in two places at once." Are you sure? We run into great contradictions when we get down to the subatomic level. In the various double-slit tests, the behavior of electrons is not only affected by observing them—they also appear to know if we're going to decide to observe them before we make the decision, showing an apparent backward causation in time!

86

Your identification with or as a material body moving through a material universe may need some scrutiny. Maybe you're here because you made a decision to observe yourself ... or because you may make such a decision in the future.

Let's move on to philosophy: Why are you here, existentially? What we're talking about now is consciousness. The currently rather popular theory that consciousness is a byproduct of physical complexity is the wishful thinking of the materialist, and materialism/physicalism no longer works as a scientific explanation. For all you know, you may have been brought into existence for a purpose. If you're here for a purpose, then your innermost desire would reflect that purpose.

- What do you want?
- What does god or your inner self want for you?
- Are they aligned?

Although we have many ways of expressing it to ourselves, I believe that everyone wants fulfillment or completion. And the good news is that it truly can be found—through self-definition, knowing what you are.

How is that possible? Your identity is inherent (essential) and immanent (within). It's not in a book, not in your attic, not on the other side of the globe, etc. It's within, close, and isn't going anywhere. You're what's aware—but you're hypnotized by the view. What will break that spell? What do you need to see or hear? "You" (the self that you think you are) can't answer that question ... only your inner self can. In the final analysis, you will have to "Let go, and let God" as the AA saying has it.

9

Longing

Longing

$\mathcal{H}$ow could we be separate from what we really are? (Think about it....) Heartache results from buying into the fictional individuality belief (FIB):

"I am a sentient creature with its personal awareness," *you say.*

"There are no sentient creatures. Awareness is self-aware," the teacher says.

"But I can't see that!" you say.

"That's because you're thinking about it, not looking at it," the teacher says.

You're conscious, and you know that you're conscious. Consciousness is like a light illuminating objects. Becoming conscious of awareness is becoming conscious of what powers that light.

There's a vibrant longing that leads us back to consciousness of awareness. It's reflected in our dissatisfaction, in our desire for unity, completion, wholeness, love, eternality....

Certain scenes or images or sounds may remind us of its existence. My personal list includes scenes of communal harmony, often associated with churches and music: A brass choir playing "Mine Eyes Have Seen the Glory" on an Easter Sunday morning in Binghamton, New York when I was eight or ten; antiphonal choirs singing in the front and back lofts of a Lebanese Orthodox church in Boston when I was a high school senior; Bach preludes and fugues vibrating the interior of a college chapel as we walked under the organ loft at the chapel entrance; a brass band standing under the dome of a Spanish mission outside San Antonio, Texas, welcoming the local people to Sunday morning mass, and so on.

We try to fulfill the vibrant longing "out there." But

its message is that an *internal* home is the place of completion, of eternality without conflict. When the excitement and adventure of traveling wears thin, it becomes more and more apparent to the weary traveler that fulfillment doesn't lie over the next hill or around the next bend. As an old hymn intones: "Come Home, come Home, ye who are weary, come Home."

Within

*I*s awareness within your body—or is your body within awareness?
Are you within the world—or is the world within you?
Is knowing that you know within knowing?
Is knowing that you're conscious within consciousness?
Or is consciousness within Awareness?

Prequel:
Are your feet down—or up?
Are they outside—or inside?
What about awareness?
Are you within your view?
If so, there must be two of you: you the viewer and you the view.
If not, then the view—including everything "outside"—must be inside, i.e., within you.

Is the Truth of your being "all-or-nothing" or "all and nothing"?

Paradigm #1: All is within. Every object of perception is within the perceiver. You are the subject, the perceiver. All is within you—you are all.

Paradigm #2: Look for your self. You are what's aware (the observer, the viewer). The view—objects of awareness—is outside; the self—the viewer, the source of awareness—is inside. What do you "see" when you look (listen, feel) within? Sound, things, etc. are observables and therefore outside. Within, you see space, silence, nothingness. That space, silence, nothingness is the source of awareness. More, it is awareness ... self-aware. It is the core of being. You are that—you are what's aware—you are nothingness.

Which is true: #1 (You are all)? #2 (You are nothing)? Both? If both, then you have a problem, a contradiction that needs to be resolved.

Does God Love Me?

A friend sent a one-line email. It was the question, "Does God love me?"
Knowing this friend, I know it's not merely an intellectual exercise but a cry from the heart.

What can I tell him, to help his cause—which means to help him find the answer for himself? It won't help, most likely, to tell him that True Love is impersonal. That doesn't assuage the broken heart of one self-identified (faultily) as a person.

It's painful to feel that longing, but the more he feels it, the closer he'll come to the answer. We can't escape the longing by going up and away from it. We have to go "in, down, and through it" in Douglas Harding's words when I asked him once about suffering. My dear, dear friend:

- ❖ All is God. Only God is.
- ❖ Love is identity, and identity is love.
- ❖ God loses himself in identification with his creature. The creature becomes his identity. He loves his creature.
- ❖ Not conscious of his identity, the creature longs for love.
- ❖ The stronger the longing, the less able the creature is to turn his attention from it, the closer he is to awakening to his identity.
- ❖ All is God. Only God is.
- ❖ God is True Love.

A Moth

9 am ...
a moth.
You know how moths are attracted to The Light,
don't you. A small number of us are drawn to the
light of an open flame ... and perish.
Of course we moths all perish, don't we.
I was ...
a moth.
When I perished
I found that my moth-body
including its moth-brain and moth-heart
was merely a cloak covering what I really am ...
Nothing.
When the moth-I perished
the flame also perished,
both flickering images eternally frozen
in the illusory movement of time.
All that remains is Timeless Space —
impossibly Self-Aware, dreaming ...
Nothing dreaming Everything.

Vertigo

*S*itting at the computer on a Sunday afternoon after having spent the weekend with friends, I tilted back my head to drink the final swallow from a can of soda. When I did, I felt as if a painless, nonphysical arrow had hit the back of my neck, and I dropped to the floor on my hands and knees in an overpowering onset of dizziness and nausea.

I crawled into the nearby bathroom and rested my head on my arms on the toilet seat. Tilting my head the least bit to the left or right magnified the misery intensely. I scanned my mental functions such as memory and computation, and failed to see any deterioration. In fact I felt extremely clear-headed. I considered crawling to a phone that was only six or eight feet distant but decided that even if I called for help, there was no way I could withstand a change of position. So I remained there as unmoving as possible for about four hours. Finally I experienced some dry heaves, and the vertigo subsided a bit. About three hours later I crawled into the nearby bedroom and got into bed, where I remained for two or three days other than to wobble into the bathroom a few times.

Gradually I recovered to the point where I used the phone to locate a doctor and make an appointment to be checked out, which was a little over a week following the incident. As I awoke on the morning of the appointment, I heard a word that sounded like *men-yair* in my mind. With it I recalled a term like "Meunière's disease" that I had read about years earlier as having something to do with the inner ear.

This was back in the days before I had an Internet connection at home, so I stopped at the local library—also before the days when Bill Gates's generosity provided computers and Internet connections there—and looked up Meunière's disease in a medical reference book. There wasn't a listing for it. In a French dictionary I found that *meunière* meant miller's wife and referred to a simple way of cooking filet of sole—but there was also an entry for Ménière's disease, which had something to do with a disorder of the inner ear, among the symptoms of which were dizziness and nausea.

After the doctor listened to my description of the symptoms and examined me, he said that without more extensive testing he couldn't be sure, but he tentatively diagnosed the problem as something to do with the middle ear, and he mentioned a Latin phrase. I then told him about my waking up with the word Ménière in my mind, and he replied, yes, that's the same thing.

I've never experienced anything like that vertigo before or since. The curious thing about it, to me, is how it came out of nowhere … and how the likely explanation for it appeared in the same way.

SOLID GROUND OF BEING

Grand Piano

I saw a video on Youtube.com of Elton John sitting
at a grand piano on a vast, otherwise empty stage,
singing and playing the song "Something About the Way
You Look Tonight," which I found was from his album *The
Big Picture.* I was familiar with the alluring melody, but I
was surprised at the opening lines:

> There was a time
> I was everything and nothing
> All in one.

Can you picture it: the sound, Elton John at the piano, the
bare stage?

Now remove the sound…
Now remove Elton and the piano…
Now remove the stage…
Now remove your birth…
Softly….

Danger of Convictions

E mail message from a college freshman after a discussion at the coffee house following one of our self-inquiry meetings:

> I just stumbled upon this quote of Nietzsche, which reminded me of this evening's discussion about political leaders and their adherence to their convictions ... "Convictions are more dangerous foes of truth than lies."

Nietzsche was right about that. When it comes to truth, what's valuable is doubt. The only thing in the way of knowing cap-T truth is beliefs about what we are. On the other hand, if we don't have "faith" or conviction that it may be possible to discover Truth or Reality, then we aren't likely to persevere. Thus conviction is what's valuable when it comes to discovering Truth! (I think we see this even in relative truth-seeking, such as with researchers who spend their lives studying proteins for clues to Alzheimer's, and so on.)

You may find that the more you penetrate into philosophical "understanding," the closest you get is to see the paradoxical nature of all things relative. The finite mind isn't capable of apprehending Truth or Reality. But the mind, with its thinking/reasoning and feeling/intuitive capabilities, is what we have to work with. We can't get to the Truth through music or mathematics, for example, but either or both could be valuable tools for improving our reasoning and intuition.

To satisfy the deep longing that propels our love of math or music, we have to get beyond the limitations of the finite mind—as crazy as that may sound.

When we're leaning in the direction of a particular belief, we need to see that its opposite may be equally valid. Then holding that opposition in our mind, we may be able to jump to the apex of the triangle of which that opposition forms the base line. That's what occurs as we retreat from illusion. Fortunately, it's not an infinite progression of such jumps.

While I have no particular interest in Marx or trips to Mars, any topic can be valuable to help people ferret out their beliefs about what they are. Our beliefs about the world or about others reflect beliefs about our self (the opposite).

Few of us are natural philosophers. We have to see that other interests are peripheral before we turn wholeheartedly to self-inquiry—and triangulating beyond all illusions about the self—as holding the most likely hope for satisfaction of our deepest longing.

Breathe In, Breathe Out

*B*reathe in,
breathe out.
Breathe in again.
Breathe out.
You're watching—that is, conscious of—your breathing during the above exercise, right?
Does breathing need your help, or has it always functioned automatically?

Think of a puppy…
a kitty…
a baby…
a tropical island….
You're watching your thoughts—mental images—during the above exercise, right?
Does thinking require your help, or does it go on functioning automatically?

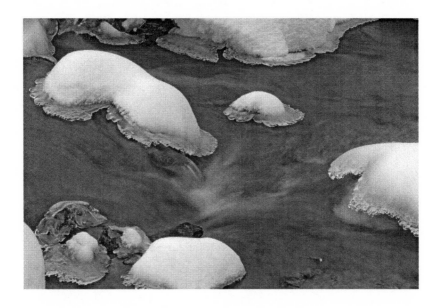

10

Getting Serious

Paean to Group Work

O healer of the gods,
 cure the earthbound humans
of their mortal status.

Monody:
The Real Self, being Nothing, weighs nothing,
while the illusory self is a heavy set of beliefs.
How can you remove the self
from blocking the view of Self?
As Archimedes discovered,
it takes a lever and a fulcrum
to move a seemingly immovable object.
The lever is relentless determination,
born of commitment.
The fulcrum is affliction to the self-beliefs,
provided by the law of the jungle.
To accelerate the process,
harness yourself to other selves
who are attempting to accomplish
the same Herculean task.
Expect the self to rebel

since the effort of self-inquiry is anti-self.

Chorus:
Onward self-inquiring soldiers
Heading in to war
With the foes of freedom
Masking what you are.

Monody:
Working closely with others will provide
plenty of irritation and afflictions to your
pride.
which can be used to broaden your view
if you don't run away and hide.

Chorus....

Monody:
If you persist to the point where you can see
there's nothing in it for the self,
the Self will take over
and finish the work for thee.

Chorus....

Eulogy:
O ghost of self, you weren't all bad or all good
but a mixture of both, like all selves,
designed to function in a dream
of perfect imperfection.

Chorus....

But Not Just Yet

"I want to awaken ... I don't want it to
take years and I don't want it quite yet."

This person has seen the enemy. He has identified with a coward masking as his friend. All his meditation, yoga, reading, and so on are designed to avoid facing what that coward tells him (and he believes) is too scary to face. So he tries to become stronger in hopes that when that scary threat to his well being finally attacks him, he'll be able to survive. By trying to run away from the supposed adversity, his suffering extends and increases. All he needs to do to end his suffering is let go of that coward. Its hold on him is the real adversity.

Dependence?

You're reading this today because you're pursuing a strategy to get what you want out of life. You may also be reading it because there's something you need to "hear." If that's the case, I don't know what it is, and you don't know what it is, so we'll have to rely on accident ... or on intelligence greater than human knowing. Would it bother you if you knew you were dependent on such an intelligence to find what you're looking for in life?

Ego

*E*go, Latin for "I am," refers to the sense of self that arises in us as young children. We gradually move away from the freedom of infancy to self-conscious inhibitions and concerns for how others view us.

Ego is a composite of desires and fears, which we identify with serially and in changing combinations. It has a rather astounding way of splitting off various fears and desires, judging them as unacceptable, and trying to dissociate from them — corralling them into what we generally refer to pejoratively as "the ego."

I-amness is the doorway through which we move from the limited self of consciousness to the unlimited Self of awareness. This transition is sometimes described as ego-death, signifying that the belief in being a limited, individual self has evaporated in the light of truth. The sense of self no longer then functions like a prism that bends the light of awareness through its facets of desire and fear.

Hunger

*W*hen you're hungry, you follow an action plan to satisfy that want. You're reading this because you have a hunger or thirst you haven't been able to satisfy. It may not be defined, but it's something you feel—an unfulfilled longing that's deeper than words. Feeling that longing, that deep want, is the starting point for going within—always come back to that. Whatever put that want there does the work of satisfying it *if you allow it.*

Everyone has a strategy they're pursuing to get what they want out of life. It may be conscious or largely unconscious. Becoming conscious of your strategy is a step in the direction of waking up. Observing it may have an impact. Part of becoming conscious of the strategy is refining your understanding of the goal it's aimed at. Cooperating with that goal is equivalent to getting out of its way.

Regarding that goal, what is it that you really want? Answering the question requires becoming aware of the goal that your ingrained strategy is pursuing. In a workshop one September, I heard several people say basically this: "I don't know what I want. I guess what I really want is to find out what I want." A want is a feeling—a feeling that something's missing, or lacking. You have to feel it … and it's unpleasant. *Knowing* what you want is an interpretation of the feeling. It comes by using the tools at hand (intuition and reason), and it provides a tentative answer to the question: "What will satisfy the want?"

I was surprised while reading *My Grandfather's Son: A Memoir,* the autobiography of Supreme Court Justice Clarence Thomas, the African-American man whose 1991 Senate confirmation hearing was such a travesty. He's not at all the stuffed shirt I thought him based on seeing newscasts during the hearings, and his book is extremely honest and revealing. Anyway, one of the things that stayed with me was his description of how, as his 31st birthday approached, he took a day off and spent it at a law library with only pen and pad. The purpose? To focus on what he wanted out of life.

If you "know" what you want out of life, you're half way there. If you "don't know," when are you going to get serious?

Getting Serious

etting serious is the equivalent of getting honest with oneself. Are you serious about finding the truth of your existence? I'm not talking about running around like your hair's on fire but of getting down to business—like Clarence Thomas did. Gautama Buddha apparently got serious when he sat down under the Bo tree; Jesus, when he spent 40 days in the desert; Paul Wood, when he put his head down on his desk and prayed for God to kill him.

Unless you spent time around Richard Rose you probably haven't heard of Paul Wood. Richard said he was one of a handful of people he'd met whom he felt certain were self-realized. Paul had grown up a fundamentalist Christian and found himself a bombardier on planes that were dropping bombs on Japan during World War II. When he saw the devastation that he was part of, all he could think of was what he'd learned from the Bible about how God was concerned with the fall of every sparrow. But where was God when the bombs fell?

Paul became unable to function and was sent home to Texas. He couldn't hold down a job there, and his wife and kids left him. He said all he could do to try to figure things out was to say the Lord's Prayer, taking it apart phrase-by-phrase and word-by-word. He eventually found work as a car salesman, but one day he was having a difficult time with a couple who were prospective customers, and he said he put his head down on his desk and prayed for death. He awoke a week or so later in a hospital, knowing the answer to his questions.

You can't force yourself to get serious. You basically have to run out of other options. As Winston Churchill quipped or complained about Americans, presumably because it took them so long to get into World War II, "[They can] always be counted on to do the right thing—after they have exhausted all other possibilities." His mother was an American, by the way.

Surveys cited by Daniel Gilbert in *Stumbling on Happiness* show that most students see themselves as more intelligent than the average student, 90% of motorists consider themselves safer-than-average drivers, and 94% of college profs consider themselves better-than-average teachers. "If you're like most people, then like most people, you don't know you're like most people," as Gilbert writes in his typically clever fashion. Are you more serious than the average seeker? Is your strategy going to keep you in the game until real seriousness grabs you?

Strategy for Knowing the Self

The strategy for self-definition requires *becoming your own authority*. How is that done? By doing it on your own? By not being influenced by others? I've known people who have followed those strategies, and I agree that they are effective—for isolating yourself from possibly useful influences. They're really two sides of the same coin, the former ("no help") motivated by pride and the latter ("no influence") by fear.

It's far better to immerse yourself with people who are striving for what you're striving for, including those who may have preceded you down the path. But carve out alone time for yourself—daily, and occasionally for longer periods.

Do you become your own authority by thinking for yourself? I used to feel that it was the solution, but when I saw that all thinking is a reaction process, I realized that thinking for myself was literally impossible. What is possible, though, is to *look* for yourself with an unbiased eye not affected by thinking or feeling.

Whatever set of fears and desires is making the most noise determines your action or inaction—until there's sufficient detachment from identifying with the view (i.e., those fears and desires). To look objectively means not flinching from the contradictions you'll see about what you believe yourself to be.

Our primary desire is for *eternal survival in a state of grand equanimity.* We arrive at that state when we realize the truth that "God loves us." The purest form of love is identity. God is all; all is God. Thus the search for permanent satisfaction is the quest for knowing the self, for self-definition.

Going Within

*I*ntuitively, the self is located within. Finding the self could therefore be described as going within. When you recognize that your hunger won't be satisfied by even the highest external games (for example, the metagames of art, science and religion in DeRopp's *Master Game*), then the only possibility for satisfaction lies within … the game of discovering what you truly are.

Going within expands the view. But since the view is not the viewer, going within expands the view of what you're not. This is what Richard Rose termed retreating from untruth about what you are. It's a journey of *dis*illusionment.

Like the zoom on a camera, when the lens is fully zoomed out, you get a close-up view. Retracting the lens expands the view. Eventually you back up to a blank wall or abyss … the boundary of the individual mind. And then a *reversal of focus* leads to a quantum jump or leap.

Speaking of focus, I hear friends who are attempting to know what they are but feel they aren't making sufficient progress say they need to focus more on self-definition. How is it done? Here's what Steve Jobs, Apple CEO, had to say in a 3/17/08 *Fortune* magazine interview:

> People think that focus means saying yes to the thing you've got to focus on. But that's not what it means at all. It means saying no to the 100 other good ideas that there are. You have to pick carefully…. Life is brief, and then you die, you know?

11

The Wager

How Can You Gauge if You're Making Progress?

*A*re you moving ... or are you just keeping busy? The journey is a chipping away at identification with what's not your essence, a backing away from faulty beliefs about what you are. An acid test: Have you seen anything new about yourself that dispels a previous belief or delusion?

What do you believe yourself to be? Until you become the consciousness that knows itself, you're stuck in the land of belief—and that's the source of your unsatisfied hunger. Fortunately, though, we're designed to look for the solid ground of certainty.

Are you challenging your beliefs about what you are? You first have to become conscious of your current self-definition then look for rigorous evidence of its validity—not what you read or someone tells you but first-person evidence that comes by looking for yourself. Admitting that you don't know what you are may be a sign of progress, but don't let it be a comfortable resting spot or insurmountable hurdle.

Why isn't everyone devoting every spare moment to *conscious* pursuit of what they want out of life? I hear friends say things like: "I don't know how ... I'm lazy ... I lack courage ... I haven't found Grace," and so on. Those are all beliefs about what you are! All you have to do is look at your complaints and excuses to find beliefs.

Other signposts of progress include satoris, natural koans, and mental processes seen in slow motion.

Another indicator is becoming less personal in your interests. We generally begin by searching for happiness (emotional) or meaning (intellectual). Later stages gravitate toward seeking truth or reality.

Satori

*A*s an example of a satori experience, after a one-week intensive early in my years of searching, I was back at work and found myself holding off something until the other workers had gone home for the day. Then I felt myself going "up" (although I was still conscious of being seated in my office) and getting a view that my mind found these words to describe: "Something IS!" I realized with amazement that for something to be, an original something had to arise out of nothing—a logical impossibility. That was my first appreciation of awe.

I felt myself seemingly going up a second time, and my mind found the following words to describe the second view: "Everything is just the way it is." This realization was actually an appreciation for the conciliation of opposites, seeing that "true" and "false" have equal validity from a view that transcends them.

The Japanese term *satori* may have been used initially to refer to realizing one's true nature, but many of the "enlightenment" accounts that have come down in Buddhist literature really refer to sudden conceptual understandings—like the "Eureka!" experience of Newton when the apple hit his head or the above pair of realizations.

As wonderful as they are, satori experiences are still partial realizations within the mind's limitations.

Umbilical Cord

A natural koan found me one time when I was on a solitary retreat. It came in the form of a question that presented itself and latched onto my mind. "What is the source of my awareness?" was the first thought I awoke with, the last thought I went to sleep with, and was rather constantly on my mind for a couple days. It was wonderful. And then late one afternoon as I sat resting on a tree stump in the woods, an answer came in the form of a quiet vision: I saw that I was attached to something bigger than myself at the end of a long string.

A few years later I heard Richard Rose say that every seeker has to find his umbilical cord, the mental umbilical cord connecting us to our source, and I knew then what I had seen.

A *koan* is a question or puzzle that's not accessible through logic. It comes from the Chinese *kung-an,* which traces back to difficult cases in early courts of law. A *natural koan* is one that grips the mind seemingly out of the blue. The question posed by the above natural koan was not big enough, in my case, for the "answer" to produce a final breakthrough. But it brought on an interim realization, or opened an intuitive connection, that may have been a necessary stepping-stone on the path.

See the January 2003 TAT Forum online magazine at www.tatfoundation.org for an inspiring essay on natural koans.

Stopped in My Tracks

*A*n earlier time when I was on a solitary retreat, it had rained for several days, and I was cold (having no heat source) and hungry (from fasting). When the rain ceased, I went for a walk and spotted a boulder on the edge of a stream with the sun shining on it. My first thought was how nice it would be to warm myself there. But then I saw a "no trespassing" sign posted on a nearby tree. My reaction was fear that an unfriendly property owner might shoot me for trespassing. I found myself stopped in my tracks on the dirt road, watching the argument in my mind in slow motion. It was like a tug of war, with the opposing contestants trying to win their side of the argument. The "team" that finally made the most noise won the argument—a very primitive operation, indeed.

Seeing it once in slow motion was all the convincing I needed to admit to myself that decision-making was something that I wasn't "doing."

If Your Strategy Doesn't Seem to Be Working

*A*t the heart of the struggle for self-realization is an opposition of wants: to be relieved of your burden while maintaining the feeling of being in charge. The feeling that you are in control, or should be, is the basic symptom of the illusion of individuality.

It's no mistake that the first step in the AA 12-step program is admitting that your life is out of (your) control. Have you reached that point of honesty yet?

If your strategy doesn't seem to be working, it may help to look at it ("Sometimes you can observe a lot by watching," as the famous yogi of baseball, Yogi Berra, was credited with saying).

❖ The mind is an *addiction machine*. Bernadette Roberts[1] at 17 was so good at disciplines that she realized the next step in discipline was giving up disciplines. (Don't overrate yourself on this!) Does your strategy condone habits?

❖ The mind's a *forgetting machine*. Gurdjieff[2] urged his students to wage a war against (mental) sleep, devising alarm clocks to awaken themselves from daydreaming. Does your strategy compensate for forgetting?

❖ The mind's a *distraction machine*. "If you throw enough mud at the ceiling, some of it will stick," as Richard Rose would tell his listeners. Does your strategy divert energy from non-critical pursuits *every day*?

---

1   *Contemplative: Autobiography of the Early Years*, by Bernadette Roberts

2   *G.I. Gurdjieff: The War Against Sleep*, by Colin Wilson

❖ The mind's a *fickle machine*. Does your strategy accommodate varying moods and convictions?

The spiritual path is contra-habit, contra-forgetting, contra-distraction, and contra-fickleness.

For years I dreamed of being an architect. I read biographies of architects, studied their designs, and luxuriated in their successes of creating beauty. But I never followed a strategy or action plan for becoming an architect. Are you merely dreaming about self-realization?

None Other

*W*hen you're aware of me
I share all your experience.
When you know me
You are none other.
What am I?

Untenable

I saw a news story one January about a 600 pound man from West Virginia who had tried and tried to lose weight unsuccessfully. He told the interviewer that he'd gotten to the point, despite the support of his attractive wife, of not wanting to live any more. Then he found himself admitting he was helpless and praying to God for help. That was 11 months earlier. By January he'd lost 300 pounds and was still losing weight!

He's an example of someone with a hunger he literally couldn't satisfy and a strategy that apparently wasn't working despite trying everything he could think of. But he witnessed a sea change in his thinking and actions when he got out of the way.

How did it unfold? First, he found his life untenable. Second, he tried everything he could think of, but all failed. Third, he admitted he didn't have will power—but he then found it within, by turning over control to something bigger than his personality.

The Wager

I have staked my body and mind
To play dice on wager with my Love.
If I lose, my Love wins me
If I win, He becomes mine.
Kabir (1440-1518)

Q: Should I make self-definition the top priority in my life? My odds of success are small, and I'm afraid I'll regret all the things I have to give up. Maybe it would be better to settle for lesser goals, which I have a higher chance of accomplishing.

Once you discover your true identity, you may see that what appears to many searchers as an all-or-nothing gamble is really a win-win decision. The odds are indeed miniscule if you don't make it your top priority, or if you don't persist, but you have no way of knowing what the odds are if you do: they may be 100 percent.

The only things you give up are faulty beliefs about what you are. Comforts, pleasures, and lesser goals can be pursued or procrastinated depending on whether they interfere with your primary goal.

What you stand to lose are impediments to knowing what you really are. Not knowing what you are ensures suffering leading to death. Knowing what you are ends suffering and brings real life. It's not an all-or-nothing proposition. What you really are is all *and* nothing.

Seeing Thought

*Y*ou may witness events unfolding in slow motion at certain times in your life. While we usually experience that phenomenon when watching something unfold in the "outside" world, like an impending car crash, it occurred twice for me when I was on solitary retreats, intent on watching the inner world of my mind.

The first occurrence had me witnessing the decision-making process in great detail—almost like watching a stage play. (See "Stopped in My Tracks" for more specifics.)

A few years later I observed the lower level thought process itself. A chain of thought begins with a percept, which then bounces off memories very much like a pinball bounces off the various parts of a pinball machine. There is only one thought-chain at a time moving through the aperture of consciousness. What was observing the process was able to follow the thought chain as it progressed but also able to look back and see what initiated it. Looking back, it could see that the percept had come through one of two channels: a sensory channel or another, undefined channel.

The most interesting part of the experience was seeing that there were two input channels of the mind—one related to the world of the senses and another that had a different source.

The experience also left me with a heightened curiosity about this: What is the nature of the "eye" that witnesses?

119

Honest Introspection

$\mathcal{R}$esponding to my statement: *"When a person real-
izes that no external pursuit or acquisition is going to
provide true satisfaction, there's only one remaining possibility, and that's going within to find what one's searching for,"* a
friend wrote:

> I don't think that can be emphasized enough.... I man-
> aged to miss the first and most basic step of honestly
> looking within and figuring out what I was searching
> for. I did a whole lot of rationalizing and intellectual-
> izing about what I might or ought to want, but I couldn't
> admit to myself ... what I was really seeing. And what
> I finally saw (and subsequently went after) was that I
> really believed finding someone that I loved and pur-
> suing something (music and a band in this case) that
> was fulfilling to me would bring me the highest level
> of happiness that was possible for my body/personality
> combo. It turns out it did make me quite happy, but I'm
> still lacking in a great and frightening way.

The path to Truth or Self-Realization relies on being honest
about what we see when we observe our interior and exte-
rior behavior. This honesty may be painful because what
we see will contradict beliefs we hold about ourselves.
Dropping the pretenses or lies will also bring a sense of
relief—of weight removed. And the unbearable burden of
separation from self will dissolve when we see through
the final self-lie.

12

Two Selves?

Panic

*H*ere's an excerpt from a friend's description of a serious and prolonged panic attack:

> Shortly after I contacted you, I had the first panic attack that I've ever had out of the blue. It was pretty terrifying... and it didn't let up for the next 4 days. During that period I was barely functional.... After those 4 days, things let up a bit. I was still anxious all the time for no reason and was miserable, but I could kind of function, but I felt like a shell of who I used to be. I felt very distant from myself. Everything felt very dreamlike and I felt like I was losing my grip on reality. My biggest fear was that I was truly going crazy and that I'd never return to normal. The thought of losing control was the most terrifying thing I've ever experienced and would send me reeling into more waves of panic.

Panic attacks often center around a fear of dying or a fear of going insane or spinning out of control. The former probably indicates identification with the body, the latter identification with the mind—the fear in either case being the loss of self.

Suppose you actually were dying or losing the self: Is there a reaction more productive than panic? The deathly fear of dying is based on a belief about what you are—an unexamined belief. ("The unexamined life is not worth living.") Wouldn't it be better to examine that belief now, when there's no panic ... and for as long as necessary until the truth is seen?

Two Selves?

$\mathcal{A}$ friend wrote to ask about an article I'd written on Common-Sense Meditation, and he included the following observation:

> One problem that I've personally run into is that during meditation, or time by myself, I can observe my self-definition receding until I'm aware of a seemingly indefinable awareness "looking out" onto all phenomena. However, I don't know who the "me" is that is aware of this seemingly indefinable awareness.

Right ... it's like when you rub the tip of your thumb and index finger together: which one is feeling which? If your attention is on the thumb, then the thumb's feeling the index finger; if your attention switches to the index finger, then it's feeling the thumb. Similarly, your attention can switch back and 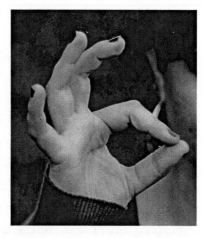 forth between the "me" that's looking out and the separate "me" that's aware of (i.e., looking back at) the outward-looking me.

We're what's aware ... alternately the thumb and the index finger, the awareness that's looking outward and the separate self that's aware of the outward-looking self. So there seem to be two me's. But we know, intuitively, that's not the case. We haven't yet located the elusive core of our being.

Depersonalization

*T*here's a human phenomenon now tagged as depersonalization disorder that leaves you feeling "as if you have no self, no ego, no remnant of that inner strength which quietly and automatically enabled you to deal with the world around you, and the world inside you" (from www.depersonalization.info). Sometimes it leads to panic attacks or depression. A friend who's been experiencing the latter result wrote:

> I've gotten so used to being in this state and not thinking about how alive I used to be my whole life.... I've already let everyone down, even if they will never acknowledge that based on what they used to think of me, as being a person that could not ever let anyone down.

He hasn't been able to see the possibility that his felt loss of self is the loss of his previous self-image. "I've already let everyone down," indicates a belief he has about what he used to be ("I'm not a person who lets people down," etc.) versus what he now believes himself to be. Our life experience is designed to humble us to the point of admitting we don't know what we are ... and then inspiring us to search for the unknown self. The flower bud obviously opens at different rates for different people.

"Don't let me down" is his current mantra and roadblock. He can't afford to feel anything positive because the subsequent letdown threatens to wipe out the remaining "me" (dismal as that is). It's a bind, and the only way out is through facing the fear.

Letting Go

I had sent a youtube.com link to a friend that shows a fellow dancing on the Avignon, France bridge to the historic "Sur le pont d'Avignon" song [Davey Dance Blog]. He replied, in part:

> It's interesting that you would email me about dancing because I've been learning how to dance in an effort to be more comfortable in my own skin and more self-confident, esp. in social situations. Dancing is also one of those things you have to just "let go" to do, and I am notoriously bad at that in just about all aspects of life. Sometimes I feel like I go through my whole life with my guard up, my fists clenched. Looking back, the few times my guard has dropped were the only times I felt truly alive. Do you think you can learn to let go?

I replied that he has a perfect analogy for letting go—the clenched fist. Letting go involves letting the muscles relax, which they obviously want to do after the contraction is seen as no longer necessary ... e.g., the adversary smiles, apologizes, walks away, lies dead, etc.

In order to see that clenching of the mental fist is no longer needed, we have to look to see why it's being clenched. It's basically a defensive response to an assumed threat. What's being threatened? The sense of self. Anything that diminishes our sense of self-importance— ridicule, failure, rejection, embarrassment, and so on— carries an implicit emotional threat of annihilation, even though logically we may see that's not the case.

The letting-go process is one of getting some distance or detachment from what we're erroneously identified with. Externally, that's the I-am-the-body belief. As we move inward, we find that we're identified with thoughts and feelings ... as when we're engrossed with a dramatic video and forget that we're what's watching, not what's being watched.

All You Need to Do

*G*uru: All you need to do is let go.
Chela: What do you mean? Let go of what?

Guru: Your faulty beliefs about what you are.
Chela: How do I do that? I don't know how.

G: Everyone knows how to let go. What prevents it is pride or fear. It's generally easier to see the fear side of the argument. What are you afraid to let go of? What is the threat?
C: Well, I'm afraid to let go of control. The fear, I guess, is that things will spin out of control ... my life will become chaotic, maybe I'll even go crazy.

G: And what are the implications of that?
C: Well, if I go crazy I won't be able to function normally, people will shun me or lock me away somewhere. I won't be able to live a productive life, to get what I want from life. I'll die miserable and unfulfilled. Even if I stay sane but things spin out of control, I won't be able to pursue what I want and may not be able to stay alive.

G: If you let go your hopes will die ... or you will die....
C: Yes, that's what it comes down to.

G: You're stuck, then, aren't you … postponing the inevitable.

C: That's how it feels. Isn't there any way out?

G: That brings us back to the solution, which is quite simple: just let go.

C: If I know how to do that, as you say, what prevents it?

G: You're turning away from the fear rather than facing it.

C: How do I do that?

G: By introspecting the mind … learning to watch the mind without getting caught up in its activity. Specifically what you'll be looking for is to observe what you actually control of the mind's operation. You tell yourself that you're in control, afraid to let go of control. Look, and see what of the mind's operation you actually run.

C: That's it?

G: That's it.

Special

*B*elieving yourself to be special is the kindergarten hurdle every seeker of self needs to clear.

Final Arbiter

*A*t the heart of the struggle for self-realization is an opposition of wants: one is to be relieved of your burden, while the other is to maintain the feeling of being the final arbiter. The feeling that you are in control, or should be, is the basic symptom of the illusion of individuality. Do you feel that you are or need to be the final arbiter in the decisions affecting your life? A very intellectual friend, who not that long before had been a staunch materialist, responded:

> I used to feel like I needed to be the final arbiter, but I've been palpably wavering on this one of late. Almost every day, there's at least one point at which I voice out something along the lines of "I'm tired of making decisions. I give up. Do whatever You want with me, and I'll take it. *I'm all Yours to play around with, and I'll be all right with all the decisions You make.*"

His capitalized "You" refers to whatever created him. Reader, you can't overestimate how relatively true his final sentence is.

Identity

$\mathcal{I}$ attended my granddaughter's high school graduation and was surprised to hear two of the three talks by graduating seniors mention the search for identity, for finding out who they really are.

Their focus, not surprisingly, had to do with what they wanted to accomplish with their lives. It was future-oriented and largely aimed at making the world a better place.

How does the search for finding out what they are sync with making the world a better place? They may intuit the path of *Yama* yoga described in Patanjali's *Yoga Sutra*, which deals with behavior toward the outside world, or *Karma* yoga as described in the *Bhagavad Gita*, which features action performed in duty or service. I obviously don't know what they have in mind, but I suspect if I talked with them, I'd find that they're trying to build a self-image that they think will be fulfilling ... that they want their actions to embrace values they think will make themselves stand tall in their own eyes—taller than others and, preferably, tallest of all.

Youthful idealism is certainly more directed toward action than is cynicism. But it seldom involves conscious action as a means toward finding our true identity. Those graduates, like most people, never admit to themselves that they don't know who or what they are. In fact, all their actions toward transforming what they believe themselves to be, or changing the world into what they want it to be, are reactions to the fear of admitting the truth.

Compassion & the Revelation of Negatives

*T*he path to liberation has one ultimate obstacle, which is our conviction of being something individual. This individuality-sense rests on the foundation of personality and our identification with personal characteristics such as compassionate or not-compassionate. Nirvana is the blowing out of this ego-flame, liberating us from the binding sense of individuality.

Progress on the path to recognition of the truth about ourselves and the cosmos is a revelation of negatives. What's what is revealed by discovering what's not. The path is one of losing illusory and delusory views. We have an innate preference for the warm and fuzzy over the cold and prickly, and much advice on how to become more spiritual is on how to add or polish positive qualities and ditch negative ones. A teacher with perspective, though, knows that Truth is reached through a successive triangulation or transcendence of opposites.

Compassion literally means suffering with. This requires personal experience of suffering and the ability to put ourselves in another person's shoes: "I've been there," or "there but for the grace of God go I." As we see more of what we're not, we become increasingly dispassionate— free from bias, objective toward our emotions, detached. We become compassionate not through acquiring new or improved character traits but through a shifting of our perspective on the dividing line between self and other.

We as the mind cannot conceive of no-mind. We as the self cannot conceive of no-self. If the mind could subtract the mind, or the self subtract the self, what would be left? Our logic tells us (inadequately) that it would be only "other" with no "me" to cognize it. The path to liberation is subtractive, but since we cannot conceive of the final removal, we try to become whole by addition, by subduing the negative and enhancing the positive. Thus striving to become more compassionate toward our fellow creatures sounds like a move in the right direction.

The ultimate compassion-trip for the ego might be the bodhisattva vow: the refusal to "enter nirvana" until all other living creatures have preceded us. This is an admirable sentiment, but what you find when you return to the center is that there are no sentient creatures, self or other. And yet you will feel great compassion for them.

Don't worry—work. Compassion and other good stuff comes as we go within. Keep your eye on the goal, which is permanent satisfaction, not temporary relief or forgetfulness. To find that, we must become permanent—which is only a question of discovering our true identity.

13

The
Secret?

Exploring and Imploring

*W*hat do you want most from your life or lack most in your life? What do you feel is the best bet or best route for getting there?

Paths in space-time are made up of discrete components. If you're on a long path, you may need milestones or other scenic markers to be able to gauge progress. If you're crossing shallow water or boggy ground, your path may appear to be more like stepping-stones. In any case:

- What do you see when you look back at where you've been?
- What's the last milestone you've passed, or the stepping-stone you're currently on?

Is there any reason or need to carve out a block of time each day to devote to the attainment of your want or fulfillment of what's missing? What, if any, value does a daily period devoted to solitary exploration (or imploring) have in your eyes or heart?

The Latin verb *plōrāre* means to weep. The word explore comes from *ex + plōrāre*, which means to cry out, as to raise game. Imploring comes from *im + plōrāre*, to entreat or beg. When it comes to knowing what we are, we may start off exploring, sending out our sight or calling out, hoping that the god or goddess of knowing may appear. Eventually we realize that we have to look inside, but we don't know how to do it. So we have no recourse but to pray within for help.

Am I the Decision-Maker?

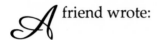 friend wrote:

I've been confused about the issue of decision-making for many years now. Yes, it looks like I might not be the decision maker based on evidence and feeling. Yet I still feel responsible for "my" decisions. Especially when something goes wrong, I feel like I could've made a better decision so as to have influenced the course of things.

I feel like the "I" that I keep referring to has got to be something. The "I" feels a bit like it's being hunted if the claim that "I am not the decision maker" is made. If I try to make progress in this direction when I feel adventurous, and decide to hunt down the "I" regardless of how it feels, I seem to get nowhere though.

Finally, whenever I stare at the question of whether "I" am the decision maker long enough, I end up with the following pattern: If not, there is no hope of enlightenment unless it's a part of the script.... this is a terrible situation.... Therefore, I might as well resort to the working belief I had about being the decision maker.

The "you" you believe yourself to be may not be in charge of pulling the puppet strings, but the real you may be.

The belief in being "something" may (you can't afford to take someone else's word for it) be the final faulty belief. Seeing the truth and admitting what we see takes us beyond the delusion. We can't think our way past the delusion, but a lot of thinking may be required before we're willing or able to stare at the truth and accept what we see. Seeing = Being.

The "I" hunting the "I" is the mind trying to see the mind. It's the way home. When or if you see that you—the viewer—are not the decision-making machinery, any other conclusions you draw from that revelation are also objects in consciousness—part of the view. You're attempting to use that questionable reasoning as more questionable reasoning to avoid the necessary looking for what you really aren't or are. Your machinery is constructed so that the more you see, the more you'll see. The motivation for continued search is not logic but feeling. The deep longing won't go away just because you see you're not the decision-making Wizard of Oz.

The deep longing is for certainty about what you really are, which the voice of intuition or nostalgia tells us solves the problem of vulnerability.

PS: If by staring at the question you mean you're thinking about it, there's a more direct way. Watch as much of the decision-making process as you're able to catch, reconstruct what you can about the mechanics that popped out a particular decision, and construct an inductive theory to explain what you haven't been able to catch … all the while hoping that some day you'll see the decision-making machinery with detachment or that the nature of its operation will become intuitively obvious.

The Secret?

I asked a friend a question, and we exchanged the following correspondence over several e-mails:

Q: What do you want (lack) most?

R: Funny I've never equated those terms before. What I want most is meaning/permanence....

What do you believe yourself to be, which lacks meaning/permanence? (Look at what you believe yourself to be. Really look, and you'll see your exact relationship to what you're looking at.)

"Really Look" implies this intensity that I haven't had in the last few weeks.... really looking is hard work.... I believe you have to live this meditation practice as a default mode in daily activity.

It's not something you can force yourself to do. It's more a question of reminding yourself what you're looking for, reminding yourself of what you're planning to look at in order to find what you're looking for, and looking with light-hearted curiosity rather than "hard work."

     The secret is 1) noticing what you're looking at, and 2) continuing to look at it—which may take many iterations—until its relationship to you becomes obvious.

This is fantastic; succinct and direct. Why has it taken years and 10,000 pages of reading to get around to accepting these facts?

The Paradox of Individuality

*W*e feel ourselves to be singular, individual, and indivisible. We see the familiar torso with its appendages extending out from our consciousness, and we observe thoughts that direct the movement of that body. We claim ownership of the body ("my body"), the thoughts ("my thoughts"), and the consciousness ("my mind"). "I am this entity, this separate and unique body-mind," we believe.

We also believe that this self came into a pre-existing world, undergoes a continuing transformation, and eventually dies. Many of us believe, in addition, that hidden somewhere in the body-mind is an invisible self, "my spirit" or "my soul," that will survive the death of the body-mind. If we try to locate that inner self, though, we run into difficulties. When we observe the mind, we see an ongoing battle among various desires and fears, which we identify with in an ever-shifting pattern: I want a piece of pie … I want to lose weight … I need emotional reassurance … I'm afraid of losing control, and so on. Eventually a decision occurs, and we identify with the "voice" or voices that win the argument. Later we may identify with one or more of the voices on the losing side of the argument, regretting the decision that we made and the subsequent action that we carried out. Introspecting the mind we see fragmentation not solidarity—a schizoid (at best) split of many selves.

"But I'm what's watching, I'm this separate consciousness, this individual observer … like you and several billion other human beings, but unique," we believe.

Discover that observer. Find out what it really is.

The Paradox of Effort

"*O*kay, I admit that I may have to work to attain what I want … but in my heart of hearts I don't want to have to exert effort. I want to attain what I want without effort or conflict, either external or internal."

Some of us have had experiences where we were "in the zone" and things just happened by themselves, effortlessly. We may have been playing a sport or a musical instrument, for example, and our performance far exceeded our usual ability. It felt great!

Some of us have had experiences where we were in the midst of doing something — making a decision or driving a car, perhaps — and suddenly we watched the action going on by itself and saw clearly that we weren't doing it. We may have been awestruck, or we may have freaked out!

If action is occurring but it's effortless — which of course is what we want — who's doing it? We tell ourselves that we're the director of our actions, that we control the decision-making process and the resulting actions. If we're not the thinker, the decider, the doer … then what are we?

"You" Can't Go There

*W*hat prevents you from being happy or from whatever you consider the *summa bonum*, the highest achievement of life? Some typical answers from friends:

- What prevents me from being happy is the threat of oblivion.
- What prevents me from knowing what I am is distraction and the ease of rationalizing it.
- What prevents me from being happy is me—not knowing what I am or what I want.

Those are the kinds of explanations we give ourselves, and the "not knowing what I am" is the closest to the simple truth, which is that the "you" you believe yourself to be can't go there. But how is it possible not to know what you really are? It results from fear of looking at your beliefs about what you are … and fear of looking at what you really are, which is "hidden" in plain view.

True happiness or fulfillment of your innermost desire appears as a result of negating unhappiness, not by incremental addition of happiness. Negating unhappiness occurs as we gain freedom from our faulty self-beliefs. For those of us who don't recognize or admit our current suffering, and those who believe we can attain happiness by acquisition, we must pursue that approach of finding satisfaction. If we do, our successes will reveal the ultimate emptiness of what we attain, and our failures will be similarly instructive; if we don't, through fear or pride, we will be stuck.

If we're willing to face our fears, then the seemingly indirect path of looking until our identity—what's looking—is known will turn out to be the direct route.

Gaining Perspective

*O*ur conversation had been interrupted when the coffee shop closed. A friend realized when he got home that he didn't have an answer to the question he had asked. So he wrote to ask again: "During your meditations, how did you determine which thoughts were relevant and which thoughts to turn your 'head' from?"

The background: He had asked about what my meditation practice had been, and I told him it was one of turning my attention away from thoughts that weren't relevant to what I was trying to find the answer to. So the question is "Relevant to what?"

Whenever we're looking for perspective, we need to go back to basics. The starting point is the feeling that's motivating our search. We feel what seems like an empty hole in the center of our being, a deep well or abyss of unfulfilled longing. The feeling generates a prayer or question that, when answered, will either move us closer to ultimate fulfillment of the longing or, finally, take us past all limitation.

When we sit down to meditate, the current form of the question or prayer is the focal point. As we're watching thoughts, we can't force them to be relevant to our question or prayer, but we can turn our head away from ones that apparently aren't.

(I have a couple friends who say that everything in their life is going fine, but they're highly interested in knowing what they are. My suspicion is that they haven't yet become conscious of what motivates their search, so for the time being we'll have to leave it as curiosity, not misery or longing.)

Pride & Precipice

Those who are superior in their own eyes,
   those who believe they're wise,
who love their intellect or intuition,
the self-righteous, the smug, the know-it-all –
these are dangling off the edge of a precipice,
and the farther up the mountain they are,
the farther they will have to fall
before they can resume their climb.

Those who are inferior
in their own eyes
are hanging off precipices
on the other side of the
mountain –
if they haven't talked
themselves
out of starting the climb.
Inferiority is the flip side
of the superiority coin.

Those who know they're
nothing special
but have an unquenchable longing
for an end to ignorance,
an end of separation from Truth and Love,
are prepared for the fall
which they won't survive.

Consciousness Never Moves

*C*onsider the possibility that no "thing" is conscious ... that things are objects of consciousness. Things come and go, are born and die. What's conscious never moves, doesn't come and go.

"That makes sense.... It would mean the source of (my) reality isn't a thing; I can get a sense that that might be a big deal in terms of my complaints," replied a friend. *"The part I have a hard time imagining is that what's conscious doesn't come and go—I can't imagine it distinct from an observation."*

That's where the problem comes in when trying to backtrack from manifestation (seeming) to being. The subject-object consciousness we're familiar with depends on manifested equipment—the body-mind—with its limitations. It's pure awareness operating in a schizophrenic mode.

"Whenever I ask myself what the source of the knowledge of observing is, my mind gets caught up in thoughts. I don't want to go on a tangent of imaginative speculations.... Do you have a suggestion on how to get past this?"

When we ask ourselves a question we don't know the answer to, we wait and watch for an answer. If the thought-stream is relevant to our question, we watch it as long as it continues to be relevant. If it wanders to the irrelevant, we can turn our attention away from it and watch for the next thought-stream. When we see imaginative speculation, we can continue to watch if it's relevant to the question or turn our head away if not. Occasionally the thought-streams may be interrupted by unexpected visions or revelations.

All the while we may recall that we're trying to look at consciousness, to know what we truly are.

Contradiction?

A friend wrote: *At some point in the past, "becoming my own authority" made a lot of sense. Now, it doesn't seem to: if ultimately I have to walk towards "giving up everything" or surrendering, that seems to conflict with the phrase "becoming my own authority." I do have the understanding that the True Me is the Real doer, etc., but since I don't actually have that perspective, the concept of surrendering versus the concept of becoming my own authority seem to be in conflict for me.*

Let me see if I can put my finger on the rationalization embedded in your question. If I could communicate it to you, I think you'd get a feeling for how you're talking yourself out of action. You've heard somebody saying something about giving up everything or surrendering as the final act in the becoming-enlightened drama. Then you hold that up in one hand while holding up in the other hand the advice to become your own authority. You don't truly know what either condition is, but you sense there's some contradiction in them. So you're going to try to understand the concepts in order to put yourself in a better position … to do what?

If you think they're possible strategies for action, consider acting on them. Try surrendering or giving up everything. If you're serious about it, you'll get to the one important thing to be surrendered, and that's the thing you believe yourself to be. If you get to that point and aren't able to surrender your self, then you may need to become your own authority … honestly admitting to yourself the truth of what you see when you look at awareness. If you do that, surrender will follow. Surrender is kneeling to the truth of what you see.

14

Relaxing Under Tension

More Aphoristics

*P*sychological fears aren't something to run away from or try to lose. Fears are there to be faced. Have you ever considered praying for more fear … and the strength to face it?

What-you-are has always known what you are. It has never changed and never will. "Becoming" (i.e., realizing or recognizing) what you are is an experience that what-you-are is having. The experience is an animated story that what-you-are has created and watches with fascination.

To become conscious of what you are, look at consciousness.

When attention is on thoughts and feelings, you're watching movement. When attention is on the self, you're watching stillness. Existence is movement, even if imperceptible (like a rock at rest). Being is absolute stillness. *Tat tvam asi.*

When you look at awareness, what do you see? Are you aware, or is awareness aware?

Relaxing Under Tension

*W*hat prevents us from seeing the truth of our being is the same as what prevents us from productive seeking: prides and fears that we become identified with. Life is set up to erode those identifications, but if we're not satisfied that life is doing the job quickly enough, then we need to find ways of encouraging irritation to the sleepy sense of self. That means a "system of work," a way of producing artificial tension—and developing the strength to hold more tension.

The ability of the mind to relax under tension is, I believe, the condition that produces revelations. The greater that opposition, the more likely the revelation will be full self-realization.

Stepping Back

A friend responded to an email with this comment and question: *"I have been thinking about your words: stepping back to get a bigger view on my dramatic life. I want to do this. What are some of the ways to do this?"*

Seekers of truth, or self, or True Self, may realize at some point in their search that they are lost in the mind. When the lens of attention is zoomed all the way out, we're lost in thoughts and feelings. The first step inward in self-inquiry is stepping back so that we're conscious observers of the thoughts and feelings ... like watching a train going down the tracks without jumping on and riding with it.

This intentional stepping back to consciously observe thoughts and feelings needs to be a daily practice. At first we may only be able to do it for seconds or minutes, and only at a time when we're not otherwise distracted. We need to work to increase the duration and then to also pursue the practice while we're engaged in activities.

We can play a game with ourselves at random times during the day by asking ourselves why we're doing what we're doing. The "answer" comes in the form of recalling the thoughts and feelings that led to the current situation and observing with some degree of objectivity current thoughts and feelings as they appear and disappear on the viewing screen of the mind.

Thoughts are relatively easy to gain some detachment from; feelings are stickier. Feelings don't disappear—as many feeling-oriented people fear. We merely escape being enslaved by them, which comes as a huge relief.

The Schoolhouse

To know the Self, we look until nothing remains to explore by looking at other than the Self. It's not something we do outside of our lives but as an integral part of our lives. Our lives are the schoolhouse. It's important to keep one foot on the ground—i.e., we live a practical life, planning for the future, and so on—while providing reminders to ourselves of our "mission."

The Self is that which "sees" itself. How do you know that you're conscious? The Real You—what you really are, always have been and always will be—is behind that: you know you're conscious only because Awareness is self-aware. And while it seems that Awareness must be hiding somewhere behind consciousness, it is "hidden" only until we lose our faulty beliefs about what we are, until we see through our faulty identifications.

The penny blocking the sun is our belief in being a separate something, an individual with its unique personality. That belief originates from our faulty interpretation of what we're always seeing. So the Truth is not hidden ... merely misinterpreted. The right interpretation doesn't come by constructing a new and better interpretation but by dropping all faulty interpretations. Life is set up to take us along that path ... eroding the ego. But some of us want to hasten the journey and can't be content until we know the truth.

The Truth liberates us from the limitations of being identified with an individual existence, with the joys and sorrows of life and death.

148

Help

*W*e all struggle so hard to find the peace-love-assurance we long for, oblivious to the fact of its immanence, its closer-than-closeness, its non-separation from us. It reminds me of living on the Richard Rose farm and tending the goat herd. Every spring the new crop of baby goats would take their turns putting their heads through the wire fencing to munch the greener grass on the other side ... then freaking out when they couldn't get their heads back through the fencing. And they'd go into varying depths of paranoid fear when we'd turn their heads to free them.

Your inner self is always ready to turn your head to free you of your imprisonment ... whenever you feel you've struggled as much as necessary and can accept the help.

The Mask

*A*t some point we need to recognize that infinite investigation, preening, regretting or tweaking of personality characteristics isn't going to take us where we want to go (Home). The personality is a mask we're looking through ... and no matter how intently we study that mask, it doesn't tell us a single iota about what we are.

Behind the mask is our individuality sense ... not to be confused with a smiling or frowning personality. Moving from an investigation of personality to an investigation of individuality is getting closer to the bone of the problem ... and the solution. We merely have to lose some of our fascination with the personality mask—and the associated psychodrama—in order to shift our focus to the bedrock conviction of individuality.

What exactly is it that you believe you are—an individual *what*? An individual *body* you may say. Do you believe you *are* a body or that you *have* a body? What has a body—an individual me-ness? If that me-ness isn't a body, what is it—is it a mind or soul? Does that mind or soul have awareness as one of its properties? Awareness can't exist without an individual body, mind, or soul, right? Or can it?

How do you know that you're aware? (Are there two awarenesses?)

What's behind the mask of personality?

What's beyond the belief in individuality?

Where the Heart Is

*R*amana Maharshi's prescription for self-realization was to ignore the mind and sink into the heart. When asked where the heart was, he referred to a spot two thumb-widths to the right of the center of the chest—not the location of the physical heart.

The literature of the Ch'an masters—the Chinese precursors of Zen in Japan—used the same word for both heart and mind: *hsin.*

Douglas Harding noted that after repeatedly doing his "driving the world" experiment—where, from a first-person viewpoint, you're not moving through the scenery but the scenery is moving through you—the scenery rushed up and disappeared into his chest rather than into his head.

If you took Ramana's medicine and followed the scenery into your *hsin,* you could return all the way Home. You may get a feeling for it when you're driving the world, but you may be able to encourage the final homecoming by allowing downtime in your schedule. For counterexample, we generally have something in mind that we need to do when we finish our daily meditation practice. What might happen if we set aside an hour or several hours after meditating to *do nothing*? (And actually did nothing, turning our head away from enticing distractions.) What might happen if we carved out a solid week or month of such days from our busy lives?

Are you afraid of a block of time to spend by yourself that's not filled with physical or mental activity? When that follows a period of intense focus, it's precisely when *going within* is most likely to occur.

Aphoristics III

*C*onsciousness is God's respiration.

*E*nthusiasm is feeling God's touch within.

*C*an you conceive of that which is its own source? Can you conceive of that which sees itself? (Hint: how do you know that you're conscious?) Are you aware? Is awareness always seeing itself?

*C*an you know/face/admit the truth if you're afraid to face the fear of being alone (The Alone)?

*E*nlightenment is seeing clearly what you've always sensed darkly. You are That which is eternally self-aware.

*A*cting without commitment is like hunting with a shotgun vs. a rifle ... good for birds, squirrels, etc., but not likely to bring down any big game.

Pride versus Honesty

*D*ouglas Harding's parting salvo to me was: "The only thing that's keeping you from the truth is pride." I didn't see what he was talking about ... but assumed it was the opposite side of the coin whose fear side I was most familiar with.

Pride has many faces, which change as we go within. The earliest is usually the family state of mind, with its component of being superior to other families in some way. Then come personal superiorities—physical (outer) and/or mental (more inner). Mental superiorities may take the form of intellectual pride or emotional pride. Emotional superiorities may be beliefs that I'm more caring or compassionate than others (that others are less caring or compassionate than I) or other forms of beliefs such as religious ones (Protestants are superior to Catholics, Muslims to nonbelievers, and so on). As we go further within, we eventually hit the pride of individuality—the painful belief in being a separate something.

The antidote to pride is honesty. Honesty is merely accepting the truth of what we see, which all the way down the line may contradict our most treasured beliefs.

Strategy? Rumi nailed it in his poem Love Dogs: "This longing you express is the return message. The grief you cry out from draws you toward union."

Trying to understand our way to truth is the intellectual path. Trying to feel our way (which goes on anyway, but below the surface for the understanding-seeker) is the emotional path. All spiritual work is a response to the feeling of our deep longing for union, for completion.

In Lambent Vesper Hue

Under the Bo tree Gautama parked,
Unmoving after years of active quest;
Refusing to move, he may have remarked,
But perhaps just taking a well-earned rest …
Since you can't summon, entice or cajole
Truth or Self to appear at your behest.

When Gautama arose, he was now whole,
The Buddha—free of longing in his chest.

At the end of the day, when work is through,
When birdsongs hush and sky glows in the west,
Dusky silence falls, shuttering the view,
Drawing us within as both host and guest.

Nostalgia speaks in lambent vesper hue:
Come home, come home; to thy real Self be true.

Wisdom Tree (Peepul; Ficus religiosa)

15

It's True

Sotto Voce

Richard Rose came out of the darkness into the light of self-realization at age 30, in 1947. I met him in 1978, five or six years after he'd established the TAT Foundation. TAT participants—mostly college students and young adults—gathered for four scheduled meetings each year in a room they'd added by their own labor to Rose's farmhouse. Richard's wife prepared food for the meetings, and for several years I manned the food counter in the meeting room. At one of those meetings I was bringing a bowl of soup from the kitchen and walking through the crowded room to deliver it. Someone behind me called out something to me, and Richard warned me: "I'm right behind you," to prevent me from turning around and possibly knocking my arm holding the soup. Then, without missing a beat, he added *sotto voce:* "I'm always right behind you."

The first vocalization was from Richard, person to person. The second was from the center to the periphery—from the impersonal core of being to its personal manifestation.

In my case, and maybe in yours, I had to hear that voice seemingly from outside myself … until, finally, I was willing, ready and able to admit the truth.

It's True

*D*o you feel you currently see the Truth, or that it's hidden from you?

If you don't see it, what do you tell yourself the explanation for the non-seeing is? Do you feel it's because the Truth is in the dark and when light reveals it you'll be able to see it? Because a new "eye" has to open in order to see it? Other?

If you do see it, do you recognize it or admit the implications of what you see? If not, how do you explain to yourself the non-recognition or non-admission?

PS: "Don't know" or "Say what?" may be accurate responses, but they merely reflect lassitude or paranoia. What are your intuitive feelings about this issue?

As a child, I held on to childish beliefs.

I was in love with sorrow.

I concocted elaborate stories to try to still the troubled waters.

I prayed to my Self, imploring my Self to show me the way, to reveal the truth of myself to myself. But when my Self asked me if I were ready, I said: "Not just yet."

I looked away and saw a projection of myself. I looked back and saw my real self.

The personal self is a clenched fist. A fist has no sight. Only the Truth sees, and only the Truth sees itself. It's true: the Truth will set you free.

Magnetoresistance

*A*lbert Fert and Peter Grünberg won the 2007 Nobel Prize in Physics for their simultaneous and independent discovery in 1988 of a quantum mechanical effect in the field of magnetoresistance. What caught my attention in the award article I read was the description of magnetoresistance: the phenomenon where the electrical resistance of certain metals decreases by an unusual amount in the presence of a magnetic field — specifically, what intrigued me was the connection between a magnetic field and decreased resistance.

The journey to knowing the self begins with the push of dissatisfaction that comes from the conviction of being an individual, and the universal reaction of trying to find something that will make that vulnerable individual self invulnerable. At some point along the way, as more and more of our faulty beliefs about what we are come into view, the motivation for the search changes. We see or feel that the problem is, and has been all along, that there is too much "self" — i.e., those beliefs about what we are. The search becomes what Richard Rose termed an "egoless vector." We no longer see anything in it for the ego-self, whose inflation is the problem not the solution, but the momentum that has built up keeps us moving in the direction of finding the answer to the "What am I?" question. Another way to describe this is to say that the movement now comes from the magnetic pull at the core of our being, which — as the nostalgia "voice" has always hinted — is leading us back to our real home.

The problem in the final phase of the search for Self is that the ego-self can't detach itself from itself. The belief in individuality can't unimagine itself. The final transition to knowing the self requires a discontinuity from the type of knowing that we're familiar with—to a knowing by identity, of recognizing our "oneness with." We've unknowingly come closer and closer to the recognition of our true identity as we've seen through the illusion of our faulty self-beliefs and, in the final hour, the magnetic pull at our innermost core overcomes the remaining resistance.

Awareness

Q: *What does becoming one's own authority mean to you?*

Response: There were several experiences in my years of self-inquiry where it felt as if an internal switch was suddenly thrown from off to on. The last one of those toggles switched my mental stance from acceptance (of Rose's explanations, or Harding's explanations, and so on) to looking for myself. I had to know for myself. This occurred during a solitary retreat. I was reviewing Harding's "testing for immortality" exercises in his *Little Book of Life and Death* and had to see for myself whether what he was describing was true. I could no longer gloss over the details. I would read a statement and then look for myself to see if I could verify it based on what I was seeing ... not thinking but actually seeing. Not seeing in a visual sense but seeing in the sense of intuitional obviousness, which includes scanning the mind for contradictory evidence. Trying to describe something of the operation may make it sound complicated, but it's not. The important part is the switch from leaning to standing on one's own. Several days followed of what seemed, in retrospect, to be intense but effortless activity. The entire focus was on looking back at what I was looking out from ... looking at awareness. And there was still something unresolved about my relationship to consciousness, which apparently comes and goes (and is not therefore immortal). On the final night of the retreat, when I had relaxed into acceptance that another retreat was over without producing finality, the open-sesame koan that had been operating during the week hit my mind one last time. The koan triggered a direct looking back at what I was looking out from, and something held that direct looking until what had been unresolved came into focus and couldn't withstand the light of truth.

Q: *Is our Higher Self emotionless?*
R: What is the relationship between you and emotions?

Q: *Can an individual be aware of two things at once? If so, does this mean that awareness has split itself?*
R: Can an individual be aware? (This question could take an inquirer all the way home.)

Losing a Coward

Q.: At the end of one of Richard Rose's university talks, a listener said: "I am afraid of losing my inhibitions. I am afraid of plunging in...."

Rose responded: "You know what you are afraid of. You think you are afraid of losing some part of yourself, but you are really afraid of losing a coward. Let him die. He is not worth the attention. There may be something magical found in the losing of that coward."

How can I let my perceived identity die?

What are the options to your retaining a false identity: To trade it in for a better false ID? To attach yourself to the identity of no ID?

The problem isn't one of specific identity (i.e., personality) but of the conviction of individuality. Rose was basically trying to shake that conviction. The shaking has to come from outside the conviction-box ... like when Arjuna's inner self manifested as Krishna, in the *Bhagavad Gita*, and shook his conviction state. Life is set up to do that if we pay attention (and sometimes even if we don't).

Become open. Look at the facts of awareness and surrender to what you see. The faulty identity dies when we see the truth and accept the implications. Are you what's aware? Is what's aware an entity, an individual something?

You can only get the answer by looking. The looking requires help from What Is, which is where praying comes in. Pride prevents effective prayer.

The Bellows

*L*ying in bed, luxuriating
in a few minutes between waking and arising,
I listen to the sound of my breathing…
Where will I be when the bellows are silent?
What will I be?
After years of searching within, I discovered the answer–
I recognized what I am
that subtends the waking, dreaming, and dreamless
sleep states, that remains unchanging with the passing of
nights and days, of seasons, of years, of life.
Life and death I now see in perspective…
And see that they don't affect me.

I Am

*I*s the practice of looking inward simply noticing that I am
aware? Do you think this is what Nisargadatta meant by
meditating on "I am"?

I don't know what he meant by that. "I am" is peculiar in that it's not an emotional feeling, not a physical feeling, not an intuitive feeling. It's the mind's reaction to the sense of self-consciousness … like the taco shell analogy that Bernadette Roberts uses. When you "remember yourself"—by noticing that you're conscious—you then have all the data you need to see that you appear to be split into two parts, and yet you don't feel like two things. Productive meditating on the "I am" would be not ignoring the disparity at the core of your consciousness.

163

Anxiety

*D*oes anxiety cause worrying
Or does worrying cause anxiety?

Behind & Within

A friend wrote: *My meditations focused on the body. I scan my body and in [Douglas] Harding-esque fashion I ask: "Is this part me?" The answer is: "No, that is out there, not in here, except for the back of my head which is behind me."*

You'd have to take someone else's word (or a mirror's word, which is the same thing) for the existence of a back of your head, wouldn't you? Where *exactly* do you witness feelings such as touching the supposed back of your head, or feeling a supposed wall with the supposed back of your head? What have you ever actually witnessed behind you?

God said: "I am always right behind you."

God said: "The answers you seek, the answers to your search for wholeness, to your questions about life and death, lie within."

The holograph asked: "Where is behind me? Where is within?"

In the Midst of Doing

*W*hen you're in the midst of doing, do nothing. Do nothing while doing. When you're in the midst of existing, be nothing. Be nothing while existing.

*I*t's only when you run out of possible ways out that you may find the way in.

*W*hen you feel *the call* of nostalgia, if you watch closely you may see the reaction that inhibits acting on it. Every second of existence is like going through a revolving door … always with the option of exiting into the unknown that's calling.

*T*he personal self is a clenched fist. A fist has no sight. Only the Truth sees, and only the Truth sees itself.

*M*ental clarity increases as we "back up" within the mind … as more and more of the mind's activity comes into view. Final mental clarity is only possible if we can see mind from a higher perspective.

16

Work,
Watch,
Wait

Home

*W*here you are lord and master,
   Where there's no maintenance,
No mortgage, no expenses,
No disharmony with neighbor, family or friends,
No burst water pipes,
No roofs damaged by wind,
No grass to mow, no carpets to vacuum,
No dishes to wash, no bathrooms to clean,
No parts to wear out and die,
No worries….

Petition

Our one father,
Please remove the cloak of faulty beliefs
About what you and what we are,
Which prevents us from acknowledging
What you and we really are.

*I*n a dream some friends and I were voicing some well-known prayer. After the 3rd line, everyone stopped & looked at me. I'd apparently gotten the words wrong. One of the friends asked me if I'd like to lead a prayer. I said no thanks, and he laughed at my response. As I awoke, I was having second thoughts about my response … thinking about a prayer I could construct for my friends. Above is the prayer that then composed itself for them.

Feeling a Path In

*W*hen the seeker gets tired of being a seeker and wants to be a finder, determination arises from realizing: "I don't want to live like this any longer ... I've got to see the truth of my existence for myself." Intuition (refined feeling) will then take us to the doorway. There will be some trigger that says: "Open, Simsim" (as opened the cave, sealed by magic, for Ali Baba) and we will be looking through the doorway into Awareness. This may occur several times. If we continue looking, we will find ourselves back Home. To get to the point of determination takes a combination of fighting and surrendering. For the left-brained seeker, surrendering may be the harder fight.

Detachment

*D*etachment occurs when we become conscious that we're watching something. That doesn't necessarily mean that the mind is going to stop its "normal" operation and attention won't ever get caught up in the view again. Those moments of consciousness are all that you can really talk about, aren't they? The rest is speculation ... like where you were during dreamless sleep. When we wake up in the middle of a meeting or class and realize we must have been sleeping, we may react with a desire, and maybe a determination, not to fall asleep again in the same situation. How do we go about that? We either have to devise a way to try to catch ourselves as we're nodding off or devise some trip-wire that will wake us immediately after we've fallen asleep. All action comes down to those moments when we're consciously conscious.

Deepest Want

The toughest thing for many, perhaps most, seekers is to be honest with themselves about what they really want. In retrospect, it seems very clear to me that our deepest "want" is the feeling of longing or incompleteness. And there's a whisper of remembrance associated with it: a vague memory of home, where everything's perfect. Feeling that feeling provides the best direction for a person's life, I believe. No two paths are going to be the same, so the feeling may lead us down paths that aren't the same as Richard Rose's or Douglas Harding's or anyone else's. But the feeling will guide us—maybe with many side paths and through potholes, depending on our ability and willingness to listen to it—to complete fulfillment.

Work, Watch, Wait

*S*o Jesus said to those Jews who believed in him, "If you live by what I say, you are truly my disciples. You will know the truth, and the truth will set you free." John 8:31-32

Chela A: What does it mean to know the truth?

Teacher: Knowing the truth is not a knowing in any form you're familiar with. It's seeing *what is* as opposed to *what seems.* "What is" is what you truly are. Do you know what you are? Do you see the truth?

A: Apparently not. I don't really know what I am, and I certainly don't feel free. So I must not see the truth.

T: What do you tell yourself the reason for the non-seeing is? Do you feel it's because the truth is in the dark & when light reveals it you'll be able to see it? Because a new "eye" has to open in order to see it? Something else?

A: I keep seeing my personal self! It's annoying. It's just a damned notion, but I take it to be so real. No, no other light, or new eye, just a stupid conviction that needs to stop happening. "Unclenching" sounds kind of like what's needed.

T: Yes, the personal self is like a clenched fist, and a fist has no sight. Only the Self sees, and only the Self sees itself. Reflecting back on my life, I could say: "I looked away and saw a projection of myself. I looked back and saw my real self."

Teacher to Chelas B, C, D and E: Do you feel you currently see the Truth, or that it's hidden from you? If you do see it, do you recognize it or admit the implications of what you see? If not, how do you explain to yourself the non-recognition or non-admission?

Chela B: I feel that I can see the Truth. I can see that all things arise and disappear in the view, including every single aspect of I/me....

I tell myself that there must be something I'm NOT seeing clearly, which is why I persist in craving, seeking and trying to become something. I don't know which of the two categories this explanation falls in, since the explanation probably contains aspects of both. I am tending toward the interpretation that if I notice what I haven't yet noticed, then the unbelief or non-admission would be impossible to sustain.

T: "As a child, I held on to childish beliefs."

Chela C: Hidden. The mind is attached to the mental drama and pretend ego-building but could tire of this and begin to turn its inquiry to the observer and over time somehow the resistance would wear out and a vision would happen that hasn't yet. I've also been assuming, since what I see isn't me, I need to see something I haven't yet, when the observation is part of the truth too. It's that kind of mental blinders (in this case a misinterpretation perhaps) that keep the view focused on the parts rather than the whole and I don't know how many are left and how long it'll take to see them.

T: "I was in love with sorrow."

Chela D: I often feel like I see the Truth. I don't fully accept it because I still have attachments to untruth. Some of these attachments I'm not seeing yet. Some I'm not willing to let go of yet.

T: "I concocted elaborate stories to try to still the troubled waters."

Chela E: It feels like it's hidden. I tell myself it's not seen because I'm not ready yet due to continued strength of the ego (individuality sense) and all its attachments. I can hypothetically understand that Truth may be perfectly obvious and I'm just ignoring it because of this. Also, the Truth as expressed by those reporting back feels extremely right, but somehow seems too good to be true.

T: "I prayed to my Self, imploring my Self to show me the way, to reveal the truth of myself to myself. But when my Self asked me if I were ready, I said: 'Not just yet.'"

Chela D: I've been working hard, writing down my observations, learning new things, etc. Is all this an elaborate story I've invented to avoid the Truth?

T: That's a question you'll have to answer yourself. You're the only authority to gauge whether my autobiographical response ("I concocted elaborate stories to try to still the troubled waters.") fits your situation.

D: Is despair a valid strategy?

T: Despair (loss of hope) is not a strategy. It's a feeling-reaction that generates a belief or conviction. The feeling is a fact; the belief or conviction is an interpretation that may be more or less valid. The existentialists like Sartre and the popular crop of today's *advaitins* (who share the view that "you're already enlightened … just admit there's no self," etc.) represent exhausted seekers who stop short of realization by latching onto the belief that there's nothing to be done. That's a premature interpretation of hopelessness. Of course some people never start seeking due to an adolescent interpretation of hopelessness ("there's no answer" or "it's too big for me to tackle," and so on). A valid strategy is to make our life a laboratory for finding the truth of what we are and to feel our way intuitively, allowing intuition to refine the strategy as we go along. Mental clarity increases as we "back up" within the mind … as more and more of the mind's activity comes into view. Final mental clarity is only possible if we can see mind from a higher perspective.

Chela B: There was a deflating effect of your statement that endures to right now. Thing is, we've done this before. The affliction, the response, the story, the forgetting—and repeat the cycle. Perhaps there is a bit more honesty, a bit more acceptance of my complete ignorance, than the last cycle. What is it that your question and feedback was designed to do? Is there a better way for me to approach this? To show that it's time that I let go of mental forms that have been repeating since childhood? But if I am convinced I am those mental forms, then how is that necessary higher perspective achieved?

T: What I said was a statement reflecting my life-experience triggered by your answer to the question. You might take a look at whether your prolonged focus on your balloon's frequent deflation is a possible defense mechanism that allows you to avoid looking at the facts that life is trying to present to you … and therefore allows a reinflating of the balloon (ego, self-belief) to prevent its collapse.

Chela E: Had a big blow to the seeker ego this past week by realizing that I'm the same old unenlightened schleb I've always been. It's like there was a house of cards being built up represented by hours of meditation, retreat attendance, doctrine study, etc., which was severely shaken and damaged if not toppled. This resulted in being distraught and a lingering feeling of gloominess. Seeking activities will continue, but I feel the grandiose ideals of

Enlightenment need to be replaced with practicality, simplicity and realism.

Recognizing what you truly are takes work—possibly years or a lifetime of work. I doubt if anyone puts in the necessary effort unless they come to see (i.e., intuit) that it's the only solution to their deepest question, desire or dissatisfaction.

What obstructs our clear view is a field of faulty beliefs about what we are. Life erodes those beliefs over time, sometimes providing traumas that knock them down. We can speed up the process by intentionally looking for them and consciously doubting them. Introspection—watching the mind's activity and looking for patterns—provides the data to challenge the validity of self-beliefs. We work then relax; pray then listen; push then wait.

We can't force a breakthrough to self-knowing. The pins have to line up properly for the lock to open, and we don't know what key will do that.

Aphoristics V

*H*ow does one straighten oneself out? By loving that which never changes.

*T*o know yourself, focus on that which doesn't change.

*A*ll seeking, mundane or otherwise, is a reaction to a feeling of want (from Middle English *wanten,* to be lacking), which in turn generates fears and desires. The deeper the feeling of want, the deeper we look for answers.

*T*here will come a time when you won't be able to ignore what you're running away from. Why put it off? Wouldn't it be better to live the rest of your life without having to be on the run?

*M*editation in a way is like clearing the room of attendees so that you can get down to business with yourself, by yourself, for and about yourself.

17

Life Is like a Flame

Life Is like a Flame

*A*nd it's going to go out, isn't it … possibly unexpectedly.

In life we find ourselves between two voids. Where were you before birth? Where will you be after death? There's no guarantee that death will bring oblivion (if that's your preference) or won't (if that's what you'd prefer).

You may be thinking, "I'm not afraid of death … just the suffering that might precede it." If that's the case, is pride then what's keeping you from facing your mortality?

Before awakening we sleepwalk through life, dreaming life. What if the dream ends before we awake?

Where do you hear the voice that's speaking to you? You have to turn your attention around momentarily to see where you hear it, don't you … to *the vast unknown within.* That vast unknown within is your essential being. And the path to it is one of increasing unknowing. The knowing mind is like a clenched fist. How can light get in? The unknowing mind is like an open hand … open to the light … an open doorway.

Going through most doorways, the knower and the known remain much as they were. Going through the doorway to your essential nature, the known and the knower remain behind.

Climbing the Slope of Anxiety

*Y*ou are that which is aware. Agree? Disagree? What is aware? (What are you?) Your belief in what you are probably lies somewhere between "this body-mind" and "this aware, featureless something." Here's the final rub: You can't picture or conceive of not being a separate something, but you can't see that separate something you believe yourself to be, either. You're seemingly *stuck in the land of not-seeing-is-believing*. Like the unchained prisoners in Plato's allegorical cave, you're hypnotized by the flickerings on the "cave wall" of the mind, which you take for reality. Those flickerings come and go … and, believing you're like what you see, you're tormented by your own assumed flickering.

The path to self-realization climbs that slope of our anxiety. Mark Twain (apparently) said or wrote: "The fear of death follows from the fear of life. A man who lives fully is prepared to die at any time." What does it take to live that way?

As Socrates lay dying after being ordered to death by the Athenian court, he gave a final instruction to his disciples. Do you know what it was? Practice dying.

Life is a prolonged funeral for the self. Death is a goodbye kiss of the self we love the most. "Obey & Appease" is the story of life at the command of desires and fears. *Nirvana* is liberation from that life, from the story of the self.

True Action

*W*hat do you want? Really want.

If you tell yourself: "I don't know," are you ignoring the feeling (want is a feeling that something's lacking or missing) or unable to translate it into an answer? If you tell yourself: "It changes," "it varies," or "there are conflicting wants," have you not admitted what you really want because you're afraid it might eliminate other goodies, or maybe you're afraid of having hope smashed because what you want is unreachable? Suppose there were no constraints….

Chuck Norris wrote in *The Secret Power Within: Zen Solutions to Real Problems*: "At heart, we all want the same thing, whether we call it 'enlightenment,' 'happiness' or 'love.' Too many people spend their lives waiting for that something to arrive—and that's not the Zen way. Zen is always on the side of action…."

That, too, I believe (i.e., that "at heart, we all want the same thing"). We're all responding to the deepest level of desire that we can conceive of to fill the want. What makes the most sense to me is a Zen-like approach, and, as Norris says, that: "Zen is always on the side of action." But what is true action?

Subjective

*R*ichard Rose gave a public talk on the theme "Zen is Action." And he laid out a Zen-like *dharma* in his personal teaching, public talks and writing. In one of his unpublished communications he described the path as "subjective, subtractive, immanent, and designed for immediate changing and becoming."

I came across a story[1] relating how Socrates was sitting near the gates of Athens and was interrupted in his thinking by two travelers. Each said he was considering a move to Athens and wanted to know what kind of city it was. The first man gave a negative description of the city he was coming from, and Socrates told him he would find the same in Athens. The second man gave a glowing review of his hometown, and Socrates likewise told him he would find the same in Athens.

Experience is subjective, isn't it. In fact, all experience takes the form of objects in our consciousness. We are the viewer, not the view (or you could say that the viewer is closer to what we really are than the view). We are the unknown subject in the subject-object equation.

If self-discovery were an objective process, we could find the truth in a book, or in our thoughts or our dreams. Neurologists search for the self by studying the brains of "other subjects" (i.e., objects). The Dana Foundation's January '09 "Brain in the News" newsletter contained an article from "In Search of the God Neuron" by Steven Rose (no relation to Richard Rose as far as I know) printed in the December 27, 2008 London *Guardian*. He cited that, of the 100 billion nerve cells (neurons) in the human cortex and 100 trillion connections between them (synapses),

---

1   In The Myth of Alzheimer's, by Peter J. Whitehouse MD and Daniel George M.Sc.

brain researchers could find no general command center. Instead, multiple, bidirectional pathways connect all regions of the brain.

Jonah Lehrer, in *Proust Was a Neuroscientist,* cited a study by Nobel laureate Richard Axel, whose lab "engineered a fruit fly with a glowing brain, each of its neurons like a little neon light" in order to study how the fruit fly was able to distinguish odors. Axel's conclusion: "No matter how high we get in the fly brain when we map this sensory circuit, the question remains: who in the fly brain is looking down? Who reads the olfactory map? This is our profound and basic problem."

The scientists are trying to study a subjective field (the mind) by an objective process (brain activity as sensory data). It's not going to work. The Great Undertaking is going within by looking within for that subject. We don't learn the truth about what we are but become consciously aware of It.

Subtractive

*Y*ou have two apples ... take away one, and there's one remaining. That's subtraction, right? Now what if you take away the last one? There's a void of apples remaining—which is bad if you're hungry. But if you have a headache and it's taken away, you're left with a void of headaches, which is good.

When you look back at what you're looking out from, you may glimpse (intuit, sense, feel, etc.) a void ... a void of things, which scares you. But all things are ultimately headaches, if for no other reason than their transience.

The path to absolute truth or self-realization proceeds by a process of elimination. Unlike objective science, mind science begins with an assumption (to state it facetiously) that, "I'm all that and a bag of chips." As we go within, our assumption progresses to, "well, I'm all that, anyway (excluding the bag of chips)" then to, "maybe I'm not all that after all," and so on. More specifically, we start with a set of beliefs like: "I'm a body with a great, if under appreciated, personality and limitless abilities."

We can tentatively conclude we're not the observable body ... the fingers and toes, and so on. But we have to concede that our consciousness may depend on body parts that we don't observe (i.e., the brain and its supporting equipment). We can come to see that we're not our thoughts, not our feelings, not the mental processes such as decision-making ... which are all observable objects or operations. But we're still left with the conviction of being a separate being, an aware something; still stuck with a split between what we are and what we know. Are you satisfied to live and die that way?

Looking back on your path to self-realization you may see certain milestones you couldn't see at the time. I'd describe those markers in terms of three stages and three gates of becoming.

Gate #1 is an intuitive recognition: "Aha ... the answers are within." This could be labeled the disciples' gate. Of the hundreds and hundreds of people whom Jesus or Gautama talked to, maybe one in a hundred or thousand picked up on their message. Jesus apparently had 72 disciples, Gautama 80.

Gate #2 is the intuitive realization: "I'm still connected to my source." It could be called the apostles' gate. Maybe one in 6 or 7 of the disciples can act in the Zen sense. Gautama had 11 *bhikkhus*, Jesus 12 apostles.

When we reach the determination that we can no longer rely on second-hand beliefs, "I won't run away or procrastinate any longer … I have to see/know for myself — now — what I am," we've passed through Gate #3. I'd call it the millionaires' gate. Maybe 1 in a million seekers persist to that point.

In the first stage of becoming, we identify with a personality: "I'm a person who…." Personality is a mask that, as the years add on, reflects more and more clearly our character traits and dispositions. In the second stage, we progress to where we identify with the individuality sense behind the mask: "I am a separate awareness." At some point during this stage our search becomes an egoless vector aimed at the truth. The third and final stage is that of Being, of self-realization. Our illusory self-definitions have vanished.

To recognize Truth or Self, we need to look for it — first noticing what we're looking at, and then determining if it's what we're looking for. If not, we move on (subtraction). Triangulation over a set of opposites is the process by which we back into Truth. The path to Truth is a voyage of disillusionment. Living life and pursuing Truth are not mutually exclusive endeavors. We live a life aimed at finding the truth about that life.

Immanent

*T*here are three words that sound much alike but have different meanings. *Eminent* means prominent, distinguished. Eminent is what you want to be. *Imminent* means pending, about to happen. Imminent is what you want to avoid or to happen, depending on whether you think it's something bad or good. *Immanent* means inherent, or within. In philosophy, the transcendentalist might say that God is above or beyond the material universe, whereas the immanentalist might say that God is within. Immanent is what you are, where you are.

Ramana Maharshi told his listeners that there are two paths to liberation: self-inquiry and submission. He advised self-inquirers to ask the question "Who am I?" once and then to let the mind remain quiet so that a true reply can emerge. He said the reply would come "as a current of awareness in the heart, fitful at first and *only achieved by intense effort,* but gradually increasing in power and constancy … until finally the ego disappears and the certitude of pure Consciousness remains."[1] I believe that Douglas Harding shared the same philosophy, although he developed specific exercises to help the Western mind do the work.

Ramana said that those who are less competent meditate on their identity with the Self. Wasn't that Nisargadatta's technique?

"My guru, before he died, told me: Believe me, you are the Supreme Reality. Don't doubt my words, don't disbelieve me. I am telling you the truth—act on it. I

---

1   Preface to *The Collected Works of Ramana Maharshi,* Arthur Osborne, editor. (My italics in the quote.)

could not forget his words and by not forgetting—I have realized."[1]

Ramana also said, to those who didn't fancy self-inquiry: "Submit to me and I will strike down the mind." I think most of his disciples followed that devotional path.

Existence is holographic. The world you experience, both outside and inside, is like a holographic projection ... a flickering picture show that you find so fascinating you've (almost) completely forgotten what you are. An interesting characteristic of holograms is that any piece of them contains the entire picture, although when projected it won't have all the detail (i.e., it won't have enough pixels per inch to be sharp and clear).

What you're looking for is always right behind you. If you were a hologram, where would behind you be?

The Self is closer than your breath or heartbeat, closer than your thoughts or your feelings, closer than your sense of I-amness. What could possibly separate you from what you are? The Self always IS itself. "Seeing that" (i.e., intuitively realizing it) is knowing by becoming.

The Truth is always in plain view, but the mind has an immense resistance to admitting the implications of what it sees. Another way of saying it is that the mind is in love with faulty self-beliefs.

Huang Po referred to the treasure house within as *the place of precious things:* "That which is called the Place of Precious Things is the real Mind, the original Buddha-Essence, the treasure of our own real Nature." When asked

---

1   *I Am That: Dialogues of Sri Nisargadatta Maharaj*

where it is, he said: "It is a place to which no directions can be given.... All we can say is that it is close by."[1]

Immediate

*B*ecoming consciously aware of what we are re- sults from a discontinuity. There is no separate self that becomes aware of itself. We recognize what we always have been. Ramana's "gradual awakening" took around 45 minutes (if Osborne got the story straight) and Harding's took 44 years (in my judgment) … but they both experienced ego death as the culmination.

If you were on your deathbed (which probably seems remote, but do you know how many people have died in the past hour? The CIA website gives a worldwide death rate of 8.23 per thousand per year, which works out to 6,400 per hour, or about 2 every second) and conscious, non-demented, and non-dopey (unlikely) … and if you felt you had some unfinished business with yourself, you'd probably want your family and friends to give you some private time to be with yourself, by yourself, right?

Seneca, the Roman philosopher-statesman, advised that: "Every day … should be regulated as if it were the one that brings up the rear, the one that rounds out and completes our lives."

Do you feel as if you have unfinished business with yourself? If so, does it make sense to wait for an optimal deathbed scenario? Meditation in a way is like clearing the room of attendees so that you can get down to business with yourself, by yourself, for and about yourself.

---

1   *The Zen Teaching of Huang Po*, John Blofeld (trans.)

If you go to the root of any problem, that's where the solution is. The problem of life is death ... the sting of the scorpion, as Nisargadatta called it: we believe we are something that was born and is going to die. (It's not true, by the way. Why do you believe it?)

We're distracted by endless sub-problems, but they all go back to a common root. Conscious dying is the moment of truth, and, as Douglas Harding wrote: "The art of living is to anticipate that moment, to die before one dies, to cease postponing one's death." One of the chapter headings in his *Little Book of Life and Death* quotes the following exchange between a Zen master and a student:

> Master Tung-shan: I show the Truth to living beings.
> Monk: What are they like then?
> Tung-shan: No longer living beings.

That's immediate becoming.

SOLID GROUND OF BEING

The End of Procrastination

$\mathcal{A}$ re you looking for *the path* or *the way* to more ad-venture, or are you looking for *the doorway* to the island of peace and perfection? That doorway is always right behind you. That doorway is always open.

The light coming from behind you strobes 40 times per second (from what I recall reading in Robert Pollack's *The Missing Moment* about the electrical impulses sweeping the brain), giving you a glimpse of the shadows flickering on the screen in front of you—the inner and outer drama of self and world. At any of those instants you can step out of that "moving vehicle" of strobing light and return to the Great Perfection of no self and no other.

Harding (in *The Little Book of Life and Death*) reminds us that every day is one day closer to the moment when we will be "whisked out of life—perhaps with no warning at all. Into what?" he asks. "Is there a more pressing, more crucial question?" And he adds, "is it possible to do some-thing now, first to ensure survival, and second to influence its quality and ensure that it's worthwhile and preferable to annihilation?"

Buddha's deathbed advice was to stop relying on second-hand beliefs about this most personal of all issues—"be a lamp unto yourself" in someone's translation—and not to dillydally about it ("work out your liberation with diligence").

Harding said that, in the face of death, he saw his main job was "to approach myself from a variety of angles, to keep coming back to the question of my *true* and *present* *identity* ... and *be with full awareness what I already am.* And that should reveal—almost as a side-issue—how perma-nent I am." (My italics.)

How do you know if you're procrastinating what

188

might be the most important job for you to tackle? If you haven't gotten serious about the question, "What do you know for sure?" you're procrastinating the search for what you want. Telling yourself, "I'm not acting because I don't know what to do or how to do it," is procrastination. (Nobody knows how or what to do when it comes to this biggest of all issues.) Trying to figure out *why* you do things that interfere with what's important to you is procrastination. Trying to figure out how you can become disciplined, for example, is procrastination—in values clarification (what's really important to you?) or in other action. Depression, hopelessness, and giving up are great forms of procrastination. Telling yourself there's something else you need to do first is procrastination. And so on, ad nauseum.

Success depends on finally *looking* for yourself. Stop taking in other people's laundry (beliefs) and do your own (question your beliefs).

Malcolm Gladwell, in *Outliers,* cited a study of the violin and piano students at the Berlin Academy of Music. What surprised the investigating team was that they found no "naturals" who floated to the top with less practice than their peers. Nor did they find any "grinds" who worked harder than anyone else yet didn't have what it takes to break into the top ranks. What distinguished one performer from another was how hard they worked … with those at the top working much, much harder.

"Does Our Brain Have a Switch that Makes Everyone an Einstein?" That was the title of an article in the Nov. 16, 2008 *Sunday Times (London),* about something that had occurred in Montana back in 1949. Wag Dodge and his firefighting crew found themselves cut off by a wildfire, with a wall of flame coming toward them at 30 MPH. They had been struggling for some time to find an escape route, but the situation was finally hopeless. Dodge apparently accepted that fact, gave up, and had a moment of relaxation ... and then had a eureka experience. He took a match out of his pocket, set fire to the grass in front of him, stepped into the cleared space, covered his face and pressed himself into the ground so that he could breathe the thin layer of air beneath the smoke cloud. The fire rushed over him and he survived. The other 13 members of his crew either hadn't heard his order to do the same or couldn't act. They all died.

There's a test — Trends in International Mathematics and Science Study (TIMSS) — given to elementary and junior high students in countries around the world every four years, and the participating countries are ranked in terms of the students' overall performance. It has a preliminary questionnaire with about 120 personal questions that's tedious, and many students leave ten or twenty of them blank. Somebody had the inspiration to rank the countries by completeness of their students' questionnaires. And what do you think happens if you compare the questionnaire rankings with the math rankings on the TIMSS? They are exactly the same, country for country down the list![1]

Is there a success formula lurking in those three stories?

Referring to being with full awareness what we already are, Alfred Pulyan, a Zen-like master who worked through the mail, wrote to Richard Rose: "There is only one way & that is to quit the egocentric position." (And he pointed out that we can't "do" it, since it would be like

---

1   schoolinfosystem.org/archives/2009/01/persistence_tim.php

deciding not to decide.) But "God will not come for you in a wheelbarrow. So face it! Either you get nowhere while you live or you do it the hard way. No 'royal' road!!!"

A friend sent me a blog article "Act of Faith" by Jim Atkinson.[1] He described himself as a recovering alcoholic of fifteen years and cited a controversy (in the 12-step groups, I guess) about whether a spiritual awakening is needed for success in that process. He was skeptical about it initially but said now, after a decade and a half of sobriety, he does believe it is. He sees in retrospect that overcoming his addiction involved "a certain tectonic shift in the psyche that had nothing to do with willpower or common sense." His conclusion included this realization: "Ironically, it was the willingness to do anything to sober up—a most pragmatic strategy—that was the linchpin of my spiritual leap of faith."

Is the *willingness to do anything* what's necessary for us to be open to help from the higher power (the Self we all have in common)? Is your pride preventing a leap of faith?

---

1   http://proof.blogs.nytimes.com/2009/01/26/act-of-faith/

18

Recovering from Un-Enlightenment

Recovering from Un-Enlightenment

*J*ill Bolte Taylor was a brain researcher in her 30s, working at Harvard, when a cerebral hemorrhage shut down most of her voluntary physical action and much of the mental activity of her left hemisphere. As a result she had a shocking and dramatically pleasant shift in her view of self and world. She lost most of her analytical ability, which also included a lot of hostility that had built up over the years, and became aware of the deep inner peace that she says her left-hemisphere brain chatter covered up. She worked assiduously for the next eight or so years to recover from the stroke, but she still has access to the view from the right hemisphere—which she associates with the Buddhist term *nirvana.*

She was able to follow the spread of the hemorrhage as it shut down cell operations in various parts of the brain. In particular, she described how, when the visual cortex was affected, she could no longer detect edges—and could no longer see where she stopped and the rest of the world began. She interpreted this as a loss of her individual sense of self and considered herself to be the new, edgeless world that she perceived.

Her experience reminds me of what I think is an interesting parallel to the *satori* experience that Douglas Harding encountered at age 33. He said that the reason it was so impressive to him was that conceptual thought had stopped, and he (like Taylor) had a profound shift in his sense of self. He was so inspired that he devoted the following decades to developing and communicating experiments that he hoped would bring others to the beatific view. Taylor appears to be similarly inspired to communicate her experience.

From my conversations with Harding and reading his books, I believe that it took his left hemisphere, or psychological understanding, forty-four years to catch up with his right hemisphere or religious revelation. And when that happened, he went through an excruciating 10-day period ending in what he referred to as ego death. I'm guessing that Taylor was similarly so impressed with the new view that it never occurred to her to ask herself who or what was viewing it … or, in Douglas's case, how it was possible for the "I am" to know that it's conscious.

I've been reading the autobiographical story of her stroke and recovery, *My Stroke of Insight: A Brain Scientist's Personal Journey*, and find it rich with material for the person trying to recover not only from a stroke but also from "un-enlightenment" or even depression. Enlightenment is a loaded term pointing to a realization that can only be cartoonishly imagined by the person seeking it. Nirvana is the "blowing out" of the faulty self-belief, or the ego death that brings us back to the recognition of our true, present state of being. The progression from delusion to essence-realization is, in effect, a recovery process.

In the first days after the stroke, Taylor learned that every effort she put forth was the only effort that was important. Her goal was to be able to get out of bed and walk, but all she could do was to rock a tiny bit in bed. So rocking in bed became the only effort that mattered. Her interim goal was to be able to sit up, but that was so far beyond her ability that it wasn't wise to focus on, since repeated failure and disappointment would lead her to stop trying. Instead she first worked at mastering the frequency with which she could rock. Then she strove to rock with enthusiasm. By the time she could rock with ease, her body flowed into the natural movement of rolling. Then all effort was put toward rolling frequently, then with enthusiastic vigor, which led into sitting up.

"Most important, I had to be willing to try.... If the boundary between what you can do and what you cannot do is not clearly defined, then you don't know what to try next. Recovery can be derailed by hopelessness."

When she returned home to get strong enough for surgery to remove the blood clot on her brain, she received 5 to 15 cards in the mail every day for that month. She'd been active in the National Alliance on Mental Illness for years, giving talks around the country, being on the board of directors, etc., and those friends and acquaintances sent their encouragements. She and her mother, who was staying with her, hung them up all over her apartment. "There is no question in my mind that it was the power of this unconditional support and love that gave me the courage to face the challenges of recovery."

The seeker of self-awareness is going for the biggest recovery of all. The unconditional support and love that I sought, that you seek, and that I believe every human being seeks, is in fact what we are at the core of our being. The spiritual "heavy" (ironically, one of the Sanskrit meanings for *guru*) or "recovered individual" automatically broadcasts that message since his resistance has been blown out. For most of us, we can feel the edge of it "coming from" the guru before we can admit that the feeling is really inside us. The guru is a projection, through our equipment, of the Truth, or True Self at the center of our being.

Most people are fortunate if in their lifetime they come into contact with one self-aware person. Seekers associated with the TAT Foundation are extremely blessed to have more than one self-aware person on their radar screens. The blips are like those cards coming to Taylor every day, reminding her inner self that she is unconditionally supported and loved—but even more precious in that their presence broadcasts the fact that what we all are *au fond* is unconditional love.

Beyond All Limitation

*T*aylor tells us that the limbic system functions by placing an affect, or emotion, on information streaming through our senses. Because we share these structures with other creatures, the limbic system cells are often referred to as the "reptilian brain" or the "emotional brain." When we are newborns, these cells become wired together in response to sensory stimulation. Although our limbic system functions throughout our lifetime, it does not mature. As a result, when our emotional buttons are pushed, we retain the ability to react to incoming stimulation as through we were a two year old.

Although many of us may think of ourselves as thinking creatures that feel, biologically we are feeling creatures that think, as Taylor reminds us. As the brain matures, we gain the ability to take "new pictures" of the present moment ... we can compare the new information of the thinking mind (cortical) with the auto reactivity of the limbic mind, reevaluate the current situation and choose a more mature response.

When we experience feelings of sadness, joy, anger, frustration, or excitement, these are emotions that are generated by the cells of our limbic system, according to

Taylor. Sensory feeling on the other hand comes through the cerebral cortex, and intuitive feeling—a "gut feeling" about something (versus thinking about it)—comes via the right hemisphere of the cerebral cortex.

"Before my stroke, I thought I was a product of my brain and had no idea that I had some say about how I responded to the emotions surging through me," she wrote. "No one told me that it only took 90 seconds for my biochemistry to capture then release me." Limbic system (emotional) programs are triggered automatically but flush through the body completely in less than 90 seconds. Remaining angry, for example, longer than 90 seconds is letting it run by choice. She observed that there's a moment-by-moment choice to hook into the neurocircuitry or move back into the present moment.

In the third chapter she describes the hemispheric asymmetries she became aware of when the left hemisphere went to sleep. "One of the jobs of our left hemisphere language centers is to define our self by saying 'I am.' Through the use of brain chatter, your brain repeats over and over again the details of your life so you can remember them. It is the home of your ego center, which provides you with an internal awareness of what your name is, what your credentials are, and where you live. Without these cells performing their job, you would forget who you are and lose track of your life and your identity."

Along with thinking in language, our left hemisphere thinks in patterned responses to incoming stimulation. The left hemisphere is the ego mind, reveling in our individuality, striving for independence. The right hemisphere is the timeless mind of the present moment, of connection of all as one.

"I morphed from feeling small and isolated to feeling enormous and expansive."

"… It was impossible for me to perceive either physical or emotional loss because I was not capable of experiencing separation or individuality."

"For all those years of my life, I really had been a figment of my own imagination."

"In the absence of my left hemisphere's negative judgment, I perceived myself as perfect, whole, and beautiful just as I was."

Taylor's experience showed her that the left hemisphere is analytical, who I am, where I live, my credentials, judgmental, hostile. The right hemisphere is the home of empathy; it thinks in pictures, gathering glimpses of information, moment by moment, and then taking time to ponder the experience. Using pictures, it was impossible for Taylor to go from the general to the specific … she had to go through countless specific pictures to find what she was looking for. It reminds me of how Temple Grandin, the high-functioning autistic woman who designs animal-handling systems for stockyards, describes the way her mind functions.

I've heard from two people who've looked into Taylor's book. One, a friend who's a palliative nurse, wrote: "I'm reading *My Stroke of Insight* … I love it!! What an amazing perspective…." The other, a yet-unmet correspondent who teaches college students about English literature, wrote: "I was disappointed in Jill Bolte Taylor's book…. She kind of rehearsed a lot of known ideas about the brain's functioning, although she obviously did add her own personal story to it. I was hoping that she would speak more about her spiritual right brain experience. I wonder if she would argue that 'mystical' experience or 'realization' is simply a product of the brain, rather than, as some may think, an act of 'God' or letting go."

They're both left-hemisphere dominant, I'd say, but vastly different in their openness to new material. One clings onto what she thinks she knows more tightly than the other. Taylor saw that the left brain makes up complete stories based on minimal data, filling in many details ... and expects the rest of the brain to believe them. She realized that there are "enormous gaps between what I know and what I think I know."

As Ch'an Master Seng-Ts'an advised: "Do not search for the truth; only cease to cherish opinions." The path to Truth is indirect. We climb that mountain by putting our cherished opinions behind. As we do so, two equally valid but contradictory ways of looking at self and world will arise—like Taylor's right-brained and left-brained or Harding's religious and psychological—and come into final opposition. And since the mind isn't constructed to see both X and not-X as true, persistence will take us beyond all limitation.

Steps of Recovery

*R*ecovery from un-enlightenment may unfold along a series of steps such as these:

1. Admitting that you don't know what you are
2. Intuiting that knowing what you are (self-recognition) is the most likely cure for your condition
3. Determining to act toward that goal
4. Slowing down
5. Opening up
6. Getting out of your own way
7. Persisting until the goal is reached

It struck me that there's a great deal of extremely practical material in Taylor's book for the seeker to apply. I've found that another book I came across, *The Secret Power Within: Zen Solutions to Real Problems* by martial arts master Chuck Norris, dovetails intriguingly with very practical suggestions for several of the steps. Here are some of the things I noted and possible questions to ask yourself or exercises that you might construct from them.

1. Admitting that you don't know what you are
… And therefore know nothing for sure, not knowing the knower.

The truth of not knowing what you are may not be obvious to you without considerable deliberation. It often takes a head-smacking affliction that shakes up your sense of self, or an extended erosion of the same, and some introspective inquiry.

What do you believe yourself to be? Have you ever tried to define what you are? The mind is structured so that we only know by contrast. There's a chasm between knower and known, for example. Anything that's known is on the side of the chasm opposite the knower.

Taylor saw that there are "enormous gaps between what I know and what I think I know." Doubting what you think you know provides you with an expanded and more objective view.

2. Intuiting that self-recognition is the most likely cure for your condition

Sometimes realizations may come to you in a flash, as if an internal switch were flipped, and other times they seem to creep up behind you and you don't see the dividing line between before and after something became abundantly obvious. You may construct a reasonable explanation, but you may also find that the explanation isn't convincing to someone else.

The way I recognize intuition is that it comes with great conviction. I was devoted to analytical thinking and seeing many sides of any argument or conclusion, so the first time a strong intuition hit my consciousness as an adult, I was amazed to see a conclusion or belief that my mind didn't have any argument with. (I hesitate to admit that I was 33 years old at the time.)

Many feeling-dominant people explain all their actions as based on intuition. And they become confused (like the thinking-dominated people) when conflicting feelings don't give them a clear line of action. If a feeling arrives with great conviction, there won't be an argument in the mind. That has both pros and cons, since our interpretation of intuitive feelings isn't foolproof. The relatively rare (I think) person who's intuitive but can check it with common-sense analysis is very fortunate.

3. Determining to act toward the goal of knowing the self

Here's where some wisdom from Chuck Norris applies. Behind all the martial arts he sees a larger objective, and he intuits that their common goal is like the goal of Zen. "At heart, we all want the same thing," he writes, "whether we call it 'enlightenment,' 'happiness' or 'love.' Too many people spend their lives waiting for that something to arrive—and that's not the Zen way. Zen is always on the side of action...."

Acting on what we intuit isn't always easy. As Richard Rose used to point out, of the hundreds and hundreds of people that Jesus talked to, only 72 of them—his students, or disciples—intuited the importance of what he was saying. And of those, only 12—the apostles—apparently could act effectively on it.

4. Slowing down

Taylor realized that: "In order to hear the intuitive wisdom of my right mind ... I must consciously slow my left mind down so I am not simply carried along on the current of my chatty story-teller," and concluded that: "In order to come back to the present moment we must consciously slow down our minds. To do this, first decide you are not in a hurry. Your left mind may be rushing, thinking, deliberating, and analyzing, but your right mind is very m-e-l-l-o-w.... Become aware of your extraneous thoughts, thank them for their service, and ask them to be silent for a little while. We're not asking them to go away, just to push the pause button for a few minutes."

What would happen if you 1) decided you were not in a hurry, 2) became aware of your extraneous thoughts, 3) thanked them for their service, and 4) asked them to be silent for a little while?

Norris came to a similar realization from his experience when learning karate. "No one, not even a lover, looks at you as intensely and closely as someone who intends to knock you out in the ring." He found that his competitors would spot any gap in his concentration and take immediate advantage of it. How do you prevent it? His first instructor gave him advice that stuck: "What you are doing at the moment must be *exactly* what you are doing at the moment—and nothing else."

He applied this lesson outside the ring as well. "Living in the present without permitting thoughts of the past or concerns for the future to intrude requires a special kind of concentration and focus. Most of all it means slowing down and opening up."

5. Opening up

What did Norris mean by opening up? On the one hand, "It means being truly open to other people, listening to all of what they are saying instead of trying to reduce their concerns to a problem that can be briskly solved." In another aspect, "It means seeing what is really in front of you without permitting other concerns to block or cloud your vision."

In your meditation or introspection, can you watch mental activity without getting lost in it? Can you notice what is in front of you (in the mind's eye) without it being blocked or clouded by distraction? This is the first gateway to "opening up" the view.

Richard Rose wrote in the section of *Psychology of the Observer* on bringing the mind under control: "Something happens after this routine is practiced for a length of time. We begin to notice a motion within the head. The physical head does not move, but we become conscious of a mental head that literally turns away from a view. When you are able to turn this internal head, whenever you wish, without any inability to continue thinking, you are half way home."

Once you're able to notice what you're looking at—i.e., to watch mental activity without becoming lost in it—the next step to opening up the view is remembering what you're looking for (your true, present identity) and being able to turn the inner head away from activity that isn't relevant to that quest.

Norris says that while doing other things his "mind will sometimes suddenly tear itself loose to dream, to fancy, to race aimlessly like a hamster in a cage, to hold internal conversations—anything to avoid the reality of the present." What does he do? He remembers his first karate instructor's advice, turning his head away from the distraction, "excluding all other thoughts from my mind."

In another section of his book Norris writes that: "The basic philosophy of any martial art is designed to bring you closer to yourself.... to help the student find the way to personal enlightenment." He tells us it requires "more than physical movement; it also demands mental concentration combined with a special openness," and if you're distracted, "You can't hope to find yourself, because your vision is blocked by a thousand seemingly all-important details." Does this sound like what you run into in your meditation practice?

6. Getting out of your own way

"One of the fundamental secrets to my success was that I made the cognitive choice to stay out of my own way during the recovery process." Taylor said she became like a toddler wanting to go out and explore. She made the choice to stay out of her own way emotionally … i.e., being very careful about her self-talk. It started coming back a few weeks after surgery, but her right mind's joy and celebration were so strong they didn't want to be displaced by the feeling that went along with self-depreciation, self-pity or depression. She also noted that: "For a successful recovery, it was important that we focus on my ability, not my disability."

Is your attitude like a toddler's, wanting to go out (or in) and explore? Are you careful about your emotional self-talk—particularly the feeling that goes along with self-pity, self-depreciation or depression?

Richard Rose used to say that our biggest impediment is the belief in our inability to accomplish. Do you see that at work in your case?

Another part of getting out of her own way meant that she needed to welcome support, love and help from others—which she said she welcomed because the ego portion of her language center wasn't functioning.

Do you welcome support, love and help from others—or are you trying to solve your problems by yourself?

❧

7. Persisting until the goal is reached

Taylor said that: "I learned that every effort I put forth was the only effort that was important." Day one … rocking was the only activity that mattered. She wanted to sit up, but knew that focusing on that goal wasn't wise because it was far beyond her ability, and repeated failure, and the attendant disappointment, would likely get her to stop trying.

Compare that with your meditation practice. Do you try to "go for broke" and then become discouraged?

She had observed that: "A lot of stroke survivors complain that they are no longer recovering. I often wonder if the real problem is that no one is paying attention to the little accomplishments that are being made. If the boundary between what you can do and what you cannot do is not clearly defined, then you don't know what to try next. Recovery can be derailed by hopelessness."

Do you use a journal to keep track of self-definition questions and progress?

Taylor's bottom line: "Most important, I had to be willing to try." Jim Atkinson, a 15-year recovering alcoholic, said it took a leap of faith (in something bigger than himself) to keep him from drinking and added: "Ironically, it was the willingness to do anything to sober up … that was the linchpin of my spiritual leap of faith."[1]

---

1   http://proof.blogs.nytimes.com/2009/01/26/act-of-faith/

What are your resistances to trying? What aren't you willing to try?

"My energy was very limited so we had to pick and choose, very carefully every day, how I would spend my effort. I had to define my priorities for what I wanted to get back the most and not waste energy on other things."

This is a doozy! Are you applying it in your recovery process?

"… I loved the feeling of deep inner peace that flooded the core of my very being."

An exercise to try, sitting in silence by yourself or with a few friends.

After leaving home to seek answers, Gautama worked diligently for years. One day he sat down wearily under a tree with the conviction that he would procrastinate no longer … and arose having become what he was looking for.

Meditation I

*A*ny meditation practice requires intentional focus to "stay in the present." The simplest practice to get a feeling for intentional focus may be to count consciously. If you can count to 10 slowly without losing track of what you're doing, you're watching thoughts dispassionately. If you can do so to 10, then you can expand it to 20, and so on. When I started swimming laps for exercise, I'd swim a few pool lengths and then have to hang onto the edge of the pool gasping for air. Eventually I could add a pool length or two ... then another ... finally working my way up to a mile (36 laps, or 72 pool lengths; 35 laps would have been just a bit short).

I didn't have any mechanical or electronic lap counter, so I had to keep the lap number I was swimming in my head. That's basically all I thought about for the entire time ... repeating over and over to myself 7...7...7, etc., then 8...8...8, and so on. I had to stay present in order not to lose count. When I did occasionally, I would still have a number in my head ... but then I would ask myself, is that the correct number, or did I add one? When in doubt, I'd always drop back a number.

So my swimming was basically a meditation-while-exercising process. Obviously it would be hard to do that while being bombarded by conversations, interruptions, concentrating on various projects, etc. Which is why staying in the present for an extended time is difficult when in our ordinary daily activity. But it was easy when swimming ... especially because I knew I'd never finish if I had to keep dropping back a number.

Zen Is Action

*B*egin with a 5-minute breath-counting exercise. Breathe naturally and count your breaths silently: one … one … one as you inhale, one … one … one as you exhale, two … two … two as you inhale, and so on. [Please give it a try before continuing. Aw, come on.]

The term Zen comes from the Sanskrit *dhyana*, which means concentration or focus. Watching as you silently count is "doing" Zen. You are watching the mind.

The ultimate goal of Zen is to become with full awareness what you've always been. A term to describe that condition is self-realization.

To know your true, present identity, you have to be in the present. Being in the present involves watching the mind without getting lost in the view. Zen action is learning to be in the present.

Remember: When you remember yourself—or notice that you're conscious—you have all the data you need in order to see a vast contradiction: you appear to be split into two parts, and yet you don't feel like two things. Productive meditating on what you are would be not turning away from this disparity at the core of your consciousness.

Zen is also about developing intuition as a more direct way to self-realization. It can't be taught, but it may awaken in the mind by years of focus.

Love

A college student's curiosity brought him into a conversation some of us were having at a coffee shop after a self-inquiry group meeting. He was an obviously bright fellow—in an intellectual sense—who was active in the Atheists, Humanists and Agnostics club at his university. Ignorance to him was a function of lacking facts and theories that explain how things work. He hadn't considered the implication of epistemology, or how we know what we know.

We can know nothing for sure until we know the knower. And that form of knowing doesn't come from studying other people or even from studying scans of your own brain activity. It comes from "going within"—a subjective process of finding an anterior point of observation from which to observe the mind.

We die ignorant if we don't know what we really are. But knowing what we really are goes beyond relative knowing to absolute knowing, which is a bugaboo for both the intellectual and the emotional believer. The intellect rightly concludes that absolute knowing is beyond its ability but wrongly concludes that it's therefore impossible. The emotional believer fears it will offend some cosmic injunction.

If you love the truth, you'll never be satisfied until you know (become) the Whole Truth. Similarly, if you love love, you'll never be satisfied until you find (become) Complete Love. Don't let your fear of tackling a seemingly impossible objective stop you. And don't let the "common sense" of cultural conditioning convince you it's foolish. After all, it's your life ... shouldn't you devote it to the deepest calling you conceive of?

Comprehensive

*C*hela: I'm aware that I'm aware.
Master: That may be the world's most perturbing conflict once one acknowledges it.

*F*rom galaxies to subatomic particles, everything's in motion ... everything except you, what you really are (which is not a thing).

*I*mmortality is a realization, not an acquisition.

*L*ooking for love is, I believe, an unwitting search for our true identity. In a way it's the opposite of trying to add something more, such as wealth, fame, accomplishment, and so on. There's a feeling behind it that the path to wholeness is by losing the self, the individuality sense.

*T*he mind is not able to comprehend the Truth. Truth projects, experiences, and comprehends the mind.

About the Author

My life progression:

Deep sleep until age 18, when my girlfriend told me I was going to be a father, which provided my

First real life-direction, followed by

Falling in love with something other than myself after our son was born. A few years later, when I was a senior in college, I encountered my

First major disturbance. I realized that I had no great talent in my field, mathematics, and felt that continuing in academia would be a false pursuit, so I was going to have to get a job and work 5 days a week for the next 40 or so years—which struck me as a horrifically boring prospect. What followed were a dozen years of what I thought of as recurring

Identity crises. I had everything that should have produced happiness—a wife I loved, kids I loved, a nice house, a progressing career—but something was missing. There was some lacking purpose or meaning. I would scan the horizon looking for what might settle my soul, but everything I considered I could fast-forward to accomplishing or attaining mentally and see that it wouldn't be enough. Then at age thirty-three I

Encountered ecstasy. (Not the drug.) I met Richard Rose, and as I listened to him talking, a brass gong rang inside me. I had never experienced anything remotely similar to that before. In retrospect, I think it announced the awakening of intuition in me. The words that formed in my mind were: "This man is telling The Truth; I've never heard it before, but something in me recognizes it!" That occurred at a meeting he attended at Ohio State University, and afterwards I went to the McDonald's in the basement of the student union with some other attendees and listened to Rose talk some more. When I left the McDonald's, all the indications coming from my physical sensations told me that my feet weren't touching the floor as I walked.[1] I had encountered my

Second and ultimate life-direction. The message that Rose had gotten across to me was that the answers lie within. Sometime in the following months I made a commitment to myself to become The Truth regardless of the cost. I pursued that objective rather whole-heartedly for the next ten or eleven years until the

Second major disturbance arrived, convincing me that there was no hope of reaching my goal. That shock dropped me into a state of

Depression, which lasted for about seven years. And then changing life circumstances freed me of responsibilities that had prevented solitary retreats during those years—and during such a retreat I experienced a

Profound self-acceptance, which lifted a huge weight from my shoulders and started me back down the path of action. The action led to starting self-inquiry meetings in Pittsburgh (PA) and, seven years later, paying a visit to Douglas Harding, who provided

---

1   See "Direction" in Chapter 6 for additional details.

An alternative paradigm for my self-inquiry, which culminated, about seven months later, with

Falling into Love—attaining the goal of self-realization, which settled my soul. Since then I've continued doing what I had been doing for most of the preceding quarter century, which is finding others to work with on what I consider to be the Grand Project of life.[1]

---

1   See www.selfdiscoveryportal.com for more information about this work.

214

Graphics Credits

Cover photo: *San Rafael Reef, Utah, by Bob Fergeson. See Bob's photo site at www.NostalgiaWest.com/.*

Jacob's Ladder logo (title page): *Represents the Jacob's Ladder diagram of the mind described by Richard Rose in Psychology of the Observer.*

Tatev Monastery (p. 2): *Embossed negative of a photo taken in Armenia by Tess Hughes.*

Nkosi Johnson (p. 3): *Thanks to Gail Johnson. For the foundation she set up in Nkosi's memory, see www.nkosishaven.co.za/.*

Aten disk (p. 14): *Akhenaten, Nefertiti and children. Wikipedia Commons.*

The call (p. 30): *From a WWI memorial by Sir John Goscombe in Newcastle upon Tyne (UK). Photo by Alice Ross, www.OnlyAlice.co.uk/.*

Fork in the road (p. 37): *Photo by author. Dead ahead: the McCreary cemetery in Marshall County, WV.*

Sun on wood plank floor (p. 41): *Photo by author.*

Gate to nirvana (p. 50): *Author's photo.*

Dress-up drawing (p. 59): *Corel-7 clip art.*

Wondering (p. 67): *Portrait by author. Subject: Ben Rainey.*

San José mission (p. 72): *Photo by author. San José is the next mission south from Mission Concepción along the San Antonio River.*

Peonies (p. 81): *Pen and watercolor wash by Mike Scherer — the state flower on Indiana Historical Bureau's website. MikeScherer.nobullart.com/.*

Critical path (p. 85): *Diagram by Todd Whittington.*

Log-flower (p. 91): *Photo by Bob Fergeson.*

Candle (p. 93): *Illustration by Jessie Willcox Smith from Robert Louis Stevenson's A Child's Garden of Verses. Thanks www.fromoldbooks.org/.*

Vertigo (p. 95): *Vertigo Swirl record label logo, used with permission from vertigoswirl.com/.*

Whirl (p. 99): *Photo by Bob Fergeson.*

Archimedes with lever (p. 101): *Mechanics Magazine, London, 1824. Public domain.*

Ego (p. 104): *Wildflower photo by author.*

Second Creek Privy (p. 114): *Photo by Bob Fergeson.*

Daylilies (p. 116): *Photo by author.*

Two selves (p. 123): *Photo by Srinivas.*

Wildflower (p. 127): *Wildflower photo by author.*

Ghost Image (p. 131): *Photo by Bob Fergeson.*

Principia: Foucault pendulum (p. 138): at the Oregon Convention Center. Designed by Kristin Jones and Andrew Ginzel. Manufactured by LTW Automation, Inc. LTWautomation.net/casestudies.html/.

Dervish (p. 141): Charcoal drawing by Bob Fergeson.

Cloister walk (p. 146): Mission San Juan Capistrano, CA, author photo.

Goat stuck in fence (p. 149): Thanks to Mark at High Hopes Gardens, www.HighHopesGardens.com/.

Bodhi tree (p. 155): Courtesy of www.NewBotany.com/.

Byodo-In Temple (p. 161): Oahu, HI. Author's photo.

Panamint Valley (p. 169): Northern Mojave Desert, CA. Author's photo.

Three birds (p. 174): Photo by Bob Fergeson.

Solitude (p. 179): Alabama Hills, CA, with son, Chris. Photo by author.

Bonsai (p. 187): Dawes Arboretum, Newark, OH. Author's photo.

Rock curve (p. 199): Photo by Bob Fergeson.

Japanese garden shelter (p. 207): Photo by author. Dawes Arboretum.

Author (p. 212): Photo by Chris Ticknor.

Lighthouse (p. 214): Madisonville, LA. Photo by Bob Fergeson.

Queen Anne's lace (p. 216): Photo by author. Source of domestic carrot.

Jacob's ladder (p. 219): Photo by Bob Fergeson. Canyonlands, Utah. See Bob's photo site at www.NostalgiaWest.com/.

Index

Don't Be Afraid

Don't be afraid to love.
Yes, it will open you to disappointments and rejections,
But it will free you from the lockdown of solitary confinement.

Behind it is the desire to become one with,
And behind that is the vague memory of where we come from
And how we got here.

We came out of Perfection, of Perfect Love,
Through the doorway of mental love,
Of being one with our mother's mind.

Then, if we were fortunate, through the transition
Of parental physical affection as we matured
Into the realization of physical separation.

We long to return to The Perfection,
But we're seemingly imprisoned in individuality,
In separation.

The return journey may take us back through physical love,
The unity of touch; through mental love, the unity of rapport;
Through cosmic love, unity with all things.

In the end, our journey from Love to Love
Will take us back to the realization of oneness with
What we always have been and ever will be.

CPSIA information can be obtained at www.ICGtesting.com
Printed in the USA
BVOW05s1850110614

356060BV00003B/607/P